The Buggy Professor's

Solutions to a Healthy Lawn and Garden

By Dr. Myles H. Bader

A Handbook for Natural Gardening

PROTECTING YOUR GARDEN
By Dr. Myles H. Bader

The garden world can harbor many foes, namely insects, weeds, and plant disease. The following information will make you more aware of the dangers that face your garden and the "best ways" to protect your precious plants. While I prefer not to use poisons and pesticides because of the environmental damage they cause, some of the information contained herein does relate to these harmful chemicals and is included for your general information.

The contents include:
- ❖ Understanding how insects work in your garden
- ❖ Distinguishing the enemies from the allies
- ❖ Controlling pests
- ❖ Winning the weeds war
- ❖ Keeping plants disease free

IT'S A JUNGLE OUT THERE
The average square yard of your home garden contains over a thousand insects and most of them help, not damage your plants. Only a small number of insects cause damage. This booklet will provide valuable information and will help you sort out the predators from the minor pests.

THE BUGGY SUSPECTS
When insect eggs hatch, they become *larva*, which are immature insects. This period is often the most plant-destructive time of an insect's life. Many insects go through a stage between larva and adult, which is when they form a cocoon or hard shell around themselves.

Insects don't eat or cause damage, during this stage and unfortunately don't succumb easily to predators or pesticides. The adult stage insects usually have wings and are at their most mobile life stage and able to move around causing widespread plant damage. Some adult insects feed on plants by piercing or rasping holes and sucking or just absorbing up the plant juices. Others insects enjoy just chew on plant parts for their nourishment.

OUTSMARTING THE CRITTERS
While insect feeding is subtle and can cause a degree of damage over time, larger critters can eliminate an entire plant — or row of plants — almost right before your eyes. You can, however, keep damage down to a minimum by getting to know their habits. The following are some of the more common critters that will invade your property.

Birds: Birds in the yard can be a mixed blessing. You appreciate their appetite for insects, but when they nibble on the plants themselves, they will cross the line and turn into a nuisance. Birds can be kept away from your plants by draping bird netting on rows of plants, covering and protecting them, while not affecting their growth.

You can startle birds with noise, fluttering objects, and anything resembling a predator, such as an owl with a movable head. Birds will catch on quickly though, so change your scare tactics regularly.

Deer: One very effective way to make your garden less appealing to deer is to install a fence that slants outward away from the garden. This type of fence can intimidate the deer by making the fence appear wider than it really is. In early spring, row covers are very effective at deterring deer and should last long enough to give your plants a head start allowing time for wild food plants to become plentiful for the deer. You can also buy deer repellents, but avoid spraying fruits and vegetables, since many of the commercial sprays contain chemicals that may end up in the food.

Rabbits: The best way to keep rabbits away from your plants is to fence them out. Since they burrow, a fence must extend underground. Try not to use poison repellants such as mothballs, since this will kill them as well as your pets and other animals. Human hair or dog hair from a dog grooming shop will repel them as well as red pepper. Sprinkle it around the boundary of a garden and replenish it every few weeks. You can also purchase commercial repellents, but here again the chemicals may get into your food.

Groundhogs: Groundhogs can climb up almost as well as they can dig, so use a sturdy 4 or 5-foot fence and bury the bottom 18 inches below ground. Bend the top of the fence outwards so the groundhog will fall over backwards if it attempts to climb over. You can also use repellents but try and use natural ones such as peppermint extract. Traps are available that capture a live groundhog, which you then release into the wild. Be sure to check with, local and state ordinances about restrictions on live trapping and releasing of wild animals.

Gophers: A protective border can be placed around your garden or spray castor oil on your plants. Wire baskets can also be placed around the plant extending down 2 feet into the soil around each plant. These are commercially available in most garden supply stores.

Mice: Mice cause the most damage to plants in the wintertime since food is scarce. They like to eat the bark of trees, which make an easy meal for them. In summer, if you have a thick layer of mulch surrounding the tree that extends up the trunk. A mouse will hide in the mulch and is able to feed undetected. Best to leave a space of several inches between the tree trunk and any mulch to deter their feeding. In winter, the snow can provide a similar hiding place for the mouse and you should consider placing a wire or plastic tree guard around the tree to provide protection.

Moles: These little critters are one of the innocent burrowers of the garden pests. They burrow in search of grubs, earthworms and other insects. While doing this they inadvertently expose plant roots or will push the plants out of the ground, both of which tends to kill the plants. The tunnels; are then used by voles and field mice to reach plant roots and even flower bulbs, which they love to eat. If you can control the grubs, you can easily control the mice and voles.

Cats: Cats that roam in the neighborhood; can be a real nuisance since they enjoy loose soil and mulch to use for their litter boxes. Garden and landscaped areas are frequently used and need to be protected by spraying occasionally with a mild solution of ammonia and water. Laying rough-textured or chunky bark mulch or even ornamental rock on top of the soil will also work to repel them. You could also lay chicken wire on top of the soil and cover it with mulch. Other methods include spreading anise oil, dog hair or shredded citrus peel to deter them.

ATTRACTING BENEFICIAL INSECTS
You can take important steps to welcome beneficial insects to your yard and encourage those you purchase to Stick around. (Note: You can buy beneficial insects that aren't already in your garden through mail-order garden suppliers.) Wait to release beneficial insects until you've seen their favorite prey in the garden. Beneficial insects will not remain if they don't find food. You can even purchase food for lady beetles from the companies that sell the beetles, which will encourage them to stay after aphid populations decline.

You can also grow some plants that attract beneficial insects. With a constant supply of nectar, adult beneficial insects can live much longer than they would without it. Shallow-throated flowers are easier for many of the tiny beneficial insects to feed from than deep-throated flowers. Goldenrod; is a favorite plant that can attract more than 75 different species of beneficial insects. Include a diversity of plants in your yard to attract a diversity of insects.

Plain different species including evergreens, and plants of different sizes and shapes. A mixture of trees, shrubs, perennials, and annuals in the yard provides lots of options for food and hiding places. Avoid using broad-spectrum insecticides. Even some organic insecticides, such as pyrethrum and Totenone, are toxic to beneficial insects. Often, beneficial insects are even more susceptible to the insecticide than pests because, as predators and parasites, they are a water source for beneficial insects. Fill a shadow birdbath or bowl with stones and water and place it near the garden. Change the water frequently to discourage breeding mosquitoes.

SETTING UP ROADBLOCKS FOR THE PESTS
Pests can't damage your plants if they can't get to them. Block their access with, simple, but effective barriers around your plants, such as the following:

Copper bands: Copper has the unique ability to repel slugs and snails. Their slimy coatings read chemically with copper, generating a toxic reaction — similar to an electric current — that sends them, elsewhere. Use copper sheet metal to fashion permanent edging around your garden beds or staple copper-backed paper (available from garden centers) to the sides of wooden planter beds.

Dust barriers; You can repel some insects with a barrier of a sharp-particle dust, such as diatomaceous earth (DE), or wood ashes- Dusts work best when dry, and you have to reapply them after a rain.

Row covers: Developed to raise the temperature around plants and extend the growing season, these lightweight air and water permeable fabrics can also keep plants relatively safe from insect pests. Cover your plants early in the season, or the insects will have a chance to set up housekeeping in the garden and thrive under the protective covering. Remove the covers from plants, such as squash that depend on insects for pollination when the plants bloom.

Cutworm collars: Make cutworm collars from empty toilet paper or paper towel rolls cut into 2-mch cylinders, or from strips of newspaper that encircle the stem completely, but not tightly, and and extend 1 inch into the soil. Place the collars around transplants when you put them in the ground.

Sticky coatings: Halt insects in their tracks by applying a sticky coating to traps that attract: specific insects. Make your own by mixing equal parts mineral oil or petroleum jelly and liquid dish soap, or purchase sticky substances at local hardware stores or garden centers. To make cleanup easier, cover the lure with plastic wrap before applying the sticky coating.

USE DUST

Insects have a waxy cuticle that covers their bodies, holding in moisture. Dusts work by disrupting the waxy cuticle, which causes the insects to dry out and die. Unfortunately, these dusts harm beneficial insects as well. Although not toxic to humans, use them with caution to avoid harming the innocent "bystanders." The most common is Diatomaceous earth (DE). DE resembles microscopic shards of broken glass, which pierce the soft bodies of insects, slugs, and snails. DE kills beneficial as well as harmful insects, so be careful where you use it. DE products can contain non-toxic bait that induces pests to eat the dust, which is also fatal. Be sure and purchase the "food grade" NOT the "pool grade."

Apply the dust to damp foliage to control soft-bodied insects or sprinkle on the ground to target slugs, snails, ants, and earwigs. Reapply after a rain. Although not toxic to animals, the dust can irritate your lungs, so be sure and wear a dust mask to avoid breathing the dust. Iron phosphate can also be used and is a mineral product, when mixed with bait, attracts and kills slugs and snails.

Boric acid: For cockroaches, ants, and silverfish, look for boric acid powder. If kept dry, the powder remains effective for years without harming animals, people, or the environment.

SOAPS AND OILS

Insects breathe through pores in the cuticle that surrounds their bodies. If you plug up the pores, the insects suffocate and die. Disrupt the cuticle with special soaps and oils result in the insect being unable to maintain their internal moisture. Soaps and oils kill a wide range of pest insects, but affect beneficial insects as well.

Oils have several drawbacks. Don't use them when temperatures are likely to rise above 90°F, when plants are suffering from drought stress, or if you have applied or plan to apply sulfur fungicide within 30 days. It will also remove the bluish waxy coating from Colorado blue spruce, so avoid using it on that species. Read the label carefully for other precautions.

Horticultural oils: Use horticultural oils in the winter to suffocate over-wintering pests, such as aphids, mites and scales on dormant fruit and ornamental trees and shrubs. During the growing season horticultural oils work against aphids, mites, lace bugs, corn earworms, mealybugs, leafinmers and many others; including tough-to-kill scale insects. Mix with water according 10 label instructions and then apply with a sprayer.

Citrus oils: The oils from the skin of citrus fruits kill a broad range of insects on contact by poisoning them. The oils continue to repel pests, such as fleas, ants, and silverfish, for weeks and are safe around people and pets. The active ingredient is d-Limonene. Look for it on the label.

Plant extracts: Many herbs, spices, and plants contain chemicals that repel or kill insects. Garlic is one of the most well-known and effective extracts against thrips and other leaf-eating insects.

Insecticidal soaps: The active ingredient in insecticidal soap is the potassium salt of fatty acids, which penetrate and disrupt the cuticle that holds moisture inside the insects. When sprayed with soap, many soft-bodied insect pests, such as aphids, dry out and die. Some pests, however, especially beetles with hard bodies, remain unaffected. Insecticidal soap is nontoxic to humans and other animals and breaks down quickly in the environment. If you use a concentrated product, dilute it with soft water before using for the best effect Hard or mineral-rich water decreases its effectiveness. Insecticidal soap also disrupts the waxy cuticle on some plants, making it toxic to young and thin-leafed plants, especially tomatoes. If yon aren't sure of the plant's sensitivity to the product, always test it on a leaf or two and allow a couple of days to pass before spraying a whole plant. Follow the label directions carefully,

Microbes
Even bugs get sick. You can use a variety *of* microbes, which are infectious microorganisms that target specific pests. The beauty of these disease-causing microbes is that they're completely harmless to most beneficial insects, humans and other animals. Microbes take time to work, but they often remain active in the environment long after you apply them. All bacteria-containing pesticides degrade when exposed to sunlight and high storage temperatures. Also, insects must eat the pesticide to become infected.

Understanding Pesticide Toxicity

All pesticides are toxic, but some are more toxic than others. Some, called "acute toxins" will poison immediately upon exposure. Others, called "chronic toxins" may accumulate in body fat or high oil content organs and reach a toxic level after repeated exposure.

Pesticides are categorized as follows:

Class 1: The most highly toxic pesticides, -their labels always bear skull-and-cross-bones and the words **"DANGER"** and **"POISON"** on the label. A special license is required for their use.

Class II: Moderately toxic pesticides. Their labels always say **"WARNING."**

Class III: Slightly toxic pesticides. The labels say **"CAUTION."**

Class IV: The least toxic pesticides; they may say **"CAUTION"** on the label.

Pesticide toxicity varies from one individual to the next and depends greatly on how you've exposed to the chemical. In some cases, such as *sapodilla*, the chemical may have low toxicity if ingested, but cause severe lung damage if inhaled. Some chemicals cause bodily harm other than acute poisoning. Treat all pesticides with respect and always read the label completely before using. Check the weather too. Don't spray or apply dust in breezy conditions because the chemical may drift away from the target area and harm nearby plants or animals. If you expect rain, don't bother to apply pesticides that will wash off before doing their job.

Botanically Correct Pest Control

Insect and disease killers that come from plant extracts are called **botanical pesticides** or **botanicals**. Derived from natural sources, botanicals aren't necessarily safer or less toxic than synthetically derived pesticides. In fact, most botanicals are broad-spectrum insecticides, which kill both good and bad bugs indiscriminately. Some botanicals cause allergic reactions in people, others are highly toxic to fish and animals, and some may even cause cancer, so only use pesticides — including botanicals — only as a last resort after thoroughly reading the label on the package. The following pesticides are listed from least to most toxic to humans:

Hot pepper wax and powder: The chemical *capsaicin* or red pepper is the active ingredient in these useful botanical products. In low doses, hot pepper wax repels most common insect pests from vegetables and ornamental plants. It doesn't cause the fruit or vegetables to become spicy hot, but instead stays on the surface of the plant where it remains effective for up to three weeks. Stronger commercial formulations kill insects as well as repel them. Hot pepper wax is even reportedly effective in repelling rabbits and tree squirrels.

Neem: This pesticide is made from the seeds of the tropical neem tree, *Azadirachta indica,* and it comes in two forms; azadirachtin solution and neem oil. When insects eat the active ingredient in neem, it interrupts their ability to develop and grow to their next life stage or lay eggs. It also deters insects from feeding. Amazingly, plants can absorb neem so that any insects that feed on them may be killed or deterred from feeding. Neem breaks down in the presence of sun and soil within a week or so. To discourage insects from eating your plants, spray neem before you see a large infestation.

Pyrethrums: These insecticidal compounds occur naturally in the flowers of some species of chrysanthemum plants. The toxins penetrate the insects' nervous systems, quickly causing paralysis. In high enough doses or in combination with other pesticides, the insects die. Powerful synthetic compounds that imitate the natural chrysanthemum compounds are called "pyrethroids."

Although relatively harmless to humans, pyrethrins are highly toxic to fish and bees and moderately toxic to birds. Pyrethrins kill both beneficial and pest insects. To keep bees safe, spray pyrethrins in the evening after bees have returned to their hives for the night and avoid spraying blooming plants. The compound breaks down rapidly when exposed to sun and air and becomes less effective if stored for longer than one year. Many commercial products contain pyrethrins.

Ryania: This pesticide, which comes from the tropical *Ryania spedosa* plant, is moderately toxic to humans, fish, and birds. It's very toxic to dogs. Seek other botanical pesticides before considering ryania.

Sabadilla: Made from, the seeds of a tropical plant, sabadilla is a powerful broad-spectrum insect killer. Some people have severe allergic reactions to the chemical. Use it only as a last resort.

Head Off Disasters Before They Strike
Keep your flowers healthy and strong: Opportunistic bugs and diseases move in for the kill when flowers are weakened by improper growing condition.

Practice good housekeeping habits in your garden: Remove dead and diseased leaves and stems promptly to get diseases out of the garden before they spread. Keep the flowerbed clear of weeds, which may play host diseases or insects. Clean and disinfect pruning shears and scissors (dip them in a solution of household bleach and water) after cutting diseased plants. If you smoke, wash your hands before gardening — tobacco can contain viruses that infect Flowers.

Shower your flowers: If you use drip-type irrigation, occasionally wash the dust and small insects off your flowers by using a spray attachment on the end of a hose. Get up underneath the leaves to knock off bugs that are clinging there,

Don't bring bugs or diseases into your garden: When you buy new plants, check them over carefully to make sure that insects or their eggs aren't lurking on the undersides of the leaves. Don't buy plants with mottled, discolored, or spotted foliage. Look for pearly clumps of snail or slug eggs when you remove your flower from its pot, and destroy any that you find. Pull off any weeds that are hitchhiking with your flower before you plant it in your garden.

Encourage natural helpers: Learn to ignore the good guys (even the creepy ones), and they'll do much of your work for you. Snakes, slugs and mice, bats, spiders, toads and lizards all eat huge quantities of bugs, if you let them.

Get rid of problem plants: Be hard-hearted and replace any flower that's a perennial problem.

Identifying the Culprits

Spotting damage on the perennials that you're working so hard to grow can be frustrating, but don't overreact. Perennials are a tough bunch. A few holes in their leaves doesn't damage their vigor and probably aren't noticeable. If you're using insecticide to control bug damage, you may actually be aggravating the problem. Before you get involved in chemical warfare, find out exactly what is causing the problem. Environmental damage often creates symptoms that look very much like disease or insect mischief. Ask yourself whether any of the following conditions may be responsible for your flowers' ill health:

Air pollution: Some flowers are sensitive to smog. Their leaves may appear bleached or distorted. If air pollution is your problem, select resistant perennials. If you live in an area where smog is a problem, ask a local nursery person to recommend resistant varieties.

Chemical damage: An herbicide is anything that kills plants, although it's usually intended to kill only weeds. Use herbicides on cool, still days to prevent spray from accidentally drifting or descending as a vapor cloud onto your flowerbeds. Swimming pool chemicals can also damage plants. Mix all chemicals away from the flowerbed and immediately put the lid back on the container to limit vapors from escaping. Symptoms of chemical damage include distorted and twisted stems and foliage, browning in an even pattern over the whole plant, or irregularly shaped brown spots.

Drought: Too little water causes plants to become warped-looking, stop growing, and develop brown tips or yellowing leaves,

Fertilizer burn or fertilizer deficiency: Applying fertilizer improperly can scorch plant leaves. Too much can actually kill the plant. Shortages of any of the essential plant nutrients can cause stunting and leaf discoloration.

Freeze damage: Frost can either blacken the most exposed parts of the plant or kill the plant to the ground. Hardy perennials usually grow back after freeze damage, but, just to be safe, protect plants from unseasonable cold spells by temporarily covering them with old sheets or blankets. Don't use plastic since frost goes right through plastic.

Inadequate sunlight: When a flower isn't getting enough light, it turns sickly pale and its stems become long and spindly. If you plant in a shady area, choose shade-tolerant flowers.

Poor drainage: Flowers that are too wet become yellowish or brown, wilt, and eventually die. Plant flowers, that are tolerant of wet conditions or improve the drainage in your flowerbed.

Salts: Salt can either, occur naturally in the soil or get carried to your garden on salt-ridden breezes, if you live near the ocean. Cars can also splash salt onto your garden when roads are salted in the winter. When salt concentrations build up, your flowers can become stunted and brown. The cure is to rinse the soil with plenty of fresh water.

Sunscald: When shade-loving flowers are getting too much sunshine, they first become pale all over and then may develop papery patches or dark, irregular burns. Move the plant to a shadier location.

Transplant shock: A recently moved flower can go into a real sulk and wilt badly. Provide temporary shelter from the sun and wind until the plant recovers and has settled into its new home. If you think that insects are eating your flowers, you first you need to identify the suspects. Don't panic when you look over the following list. Most insect infestations are localized — you aren't likely to ever get to know all these pests, unless you move around quite a bit. Insects also have good and bad seasons. You may be thoroughly plagued by leafhoppers one year but not find a single one the next. The following list describes the most common insect pests of perennial gardens.

Aphids: Often, the first indication of aphid infestation is an odd twisting and distortion of the foliage.

Beetles: Many types of beetles eat perennials; many other types eat bugs. If you catch them in the act, you can tell the difference.

Caterpillars: Usually, butterfly caterpillars ate big, brightly colored, and travel alone. You may decide to look the other way when one of these critters inches by. Other types run in packs and do a great deal of damage munching on leaves and flower buds. Still another type of caterpillar, called *borers* will tunnel destructively through stems or roots. *Cutworms* are soil-dwelling caterpillars, which are able to cut off whole young plants at ground level.

Leafhoppers: These insect carry a disease called *aster yellows,* which does particularly bad things to flowers.

Leaf miners: Leaf miners are tiny fly maggots that tunnel in leaves, resulting in telltale trails.
Mealy bugs: Furry little white, oval-shaped critters, mealy bugs would be cute if they didn't do so much damage and multiply so rapidly.

Spider mites: As their name implies, spider mites are actually tiny arachnids, not true insects. Usually, the first hint of a spider mite invasion is a mottled bronze tint to the foliage. A closer look reveals traveling dots about the size of the period at the end of this sentence.

Thrips: If your flowers turn brown and are distorted and streaked with silver, tiny thrips are the culprit.

Weevils: Beetles with long snouts, weevils often drill holes in flower buds, so the flowers don't open properly, if at all.

Whiteflies: Small, snow-white whiteflies suck plant juices and reproduce at lightning speed. Symptoms of whitefly attack are mottled and yellowed leaves.

Outsmarting Pests and Diseases
Annuals are often called the racehorse$ of flowers. Few other plants grow so fast and provide so much color so quickly. But that speed can be both a blessing and a curse when dealing with insects and diseases:

The blessing: Many annuals grow so fast that they can actually outdistance problems before the problems really get a chance to set in. Vigorous, healthy growth of annuals is of itself one of the best ways to fend off many pests. Healthy annuals are less susceptible to insects and diseases.

The curse: The same fast growth that can outpace some pests is particularly attractive to others. Aphids, for example, are very fond of young tender growth. Also, the fact that annuals are often grown in masses of just one kind creates an ideal breeding ground for pests drawn to that particular food source. And if the pests get out of hand, they can rum the entire bed. But fear not, if you choose adaptable annuals (those that can grow in a variety of conditions and climates), care for them properly and observe them carefully, few problems will actually send you to your neighborhood nursery for help.

When Bad Bugs Happen to Nice Gardens

Actually, bugs are neither bad nor good. They just do what they're programmed to do: eat, grow, and reproduce. The only problem comes in when bugs and gardeners want to enjoy the same flowers. A little conflict of interest, you might say! A bug becomes a pest only if it meets both these criteria:

- ❖ It wants to eat what you're trying to grow.
- ❖ The damage it causes makes the plant look unsightly and decline in health.

An errant grasshopper may not be cause for concern, but if that same grasshopper brings along his brothers, sisters, and cousins to join in on the zinnia feast at your expense, he becomes a pest. When you start seeing a number of the same type of insects in your garden, and you notice that their activity is focused on certain plants, you need to act quickly and decisively.

When Insects Snack on your Annuals

Here are the most common insect pests that are likely to infest your annuals:

Aphids: These tiny, pear-shaped pests congregate on new growth and flower buds, sucking plant sap with their needlelike noses, and leaving a sticky sap behind that may turn black with sooty mold. Heavy infestations can cause distorted growth and weaken plants. Vinca and cosmos are two annuals that aphids commonly attack.

Geranium budworms: These frustrating pests love geraniums, nicotiana, ageratum, and petunias. The small caterpillars bore into flower buds and eat the flowers before they open, or they simply feed on open blooms. The result is no flowers, only leaves. To confirm the presence of these heartless monsters, look for small holes in geranium blossoms or the tiny black droppings that the caterpillars leave behind. You may also see the worms on the flowers.

Japanese beetles: Especially troublesome cast of the Mississippi River, these /2-inch copper and metallic green pests Feed on both flowers and foliage, often skeletonizing leaves. They particularly love zinnias and marigolds.

Cutworms: These 2-inch-long, grayish caterpillars emerge during spring and early summer nights to eat young seedling stems, causing them to fall over like small timbers. They also move on to older plants and feed on leaves and flowers.

Snails and slugs: These soft-bodied mollusks feed on tender leaves and flowers during the cool of the night or during rainy weather. Snails have shells; slugs don't. Both proliferate in damp areas, hiding under boards, mulch, and other garden debris.

Spider mites: You can barely see these tiny arachnids without a magnifying glass, but if the population gets big enough, you can see their fine webbing beneath the leaves. As they suck plant juices, the leaves become yellowish, with silvery stippling or sheen. If things get really bad, the plant may start dropping leaves. Mites are most common in hot, dry summer climates and on dusty plants. Marigolds and columbines are commonly infested.

Thrips: Another nearly invisible troublemaker; thrips feed on flower petals causing them to be discolored and the buds to be deformed as they open. Thrips also feed on leaves giving the foliage a deformed and stippled look. (You can distinguish thrips from spider mites by the small fecal pellets that thrips leave behind.)

Whiteflies: Looking like small white gnats, whiteflies suck plant juices and can proliferate in warm climates and greenhouses. They tend to congregate on the undersides of leaves.

When the Flower Bed Becomes a Sick Bed
Only a few diseases are really troublesome for annual flowers. You can prevent or at lease reduce the diseases in severity by observing good cultural practices such as planting resistant varieties or choosing another plant if you know that a certain disease is a problem in your area.

When Summer Oil Lies Dormant
Summer oil is a highly refined pesticide that works well for annuals. The words highly refined, in this case, mean that the sulfur and other components of the oil that damage the plant are removed. It is relatively nontoxic and short-lived. When you spray summer oil on a plant it smothers insect pests and their eggs. Use it to control aphids, mites, thrips, and certain caterpillars.

Don't confuse summer oil with dormant oil. You apply dormant oil to leafless trees and shrubs during winter; however, using it on your annuals will fry them. Double-check the product label to make sure that you can use the oil on annual flowers during the growing season. Then follow the mixing instructions carefully. Water the plants before and after applying summer oil, and to avoid damaging plant leaves, don't spray if temperatures are likely to rise above 85°F (29°C).

Minimizing Pests and Diseases

Flowering bulbs are tough plants and often provide years of outstanding garden service with truly a minimum of trouble from pests and diseases. The good news is that even if you do run into little problems, you can usually handle them easily with a variety of methods. However, the garden, being a garden, will sooner or later run into some sort of difficulty.

Practicing Prevention First

Before getting to the nitty-gritty of diagnosing and solving disease and pest problems, we take a look at how to avoid the trouble in the first place. Some of the following are specific tips about bulbs and others you'll recognize as good gardening practices that benefit all the plants you grow:

Start with high-quality, healthy bulbs: Choose firm, plump bulbs. Avoid those showing any signs of molds, soft rots, or insect damage. Plant the bulbs as soon as possible and at the proper time.

Store your bulbs properly

Give bulbs the conditions they need: Bulbs need proper drainage, soil, light, air circulation, and nutrition. Match the right bulb with the right conditions. Do your homework before you buy.

Water carefully to avoid wetting the leaves: Wet leaves may lead to mildew and other problems. Water early in the day or use a device such as a drip hose to wet the soil and not the foliage.

Keep your garden ship-shape: Be a detective. By keeping an eye on your garden (the experts call this *scouting),* you can spot and correct problems early, before they get bad.

Arming your Bulbs Against Bugs

When protecting your bulbs against pesky bugs, yon have several options:

Enlist the good guys: Lots of garden critters that hang around actually prey upon the bad bugs that harm plants. In a garden with a variety of plants and no pesticides, good and bad bugs co-exist in a natural balance. If the bad gays get a bit out of hand, you can bring in these reinforcements:

Green lacewings: Buy lacewings eggs and larvae to spread throughout your garden. The larvae consume aphids voraciously, sometimes carrying the remains of their victims on their backs. The adult lacewings feed on nectar and pollen.

Lady beetles or ladybugs: These familiar bugs feed on aphids, mites, and thrips. You can buy mesh bags with hundreds of ladybeetles and release them with the hope that they stick around.

Parasitic nematodes: These microscopic worms handle some soil pests, burrowing insects, and grubs.

Praying mantises: These giants of the good bug army do serious damage to aphids, caterpillars, leafhoppers, and the like. You can buy a cocoon-like sack with praying mantis eggs inside; however, you have no guarantee that the mantises will remain in your garden.

Call up the organic cavalry: If problems persist after prevention and signing on the good bug infantry, your next step is safe, organic, biodegradable controls. These methods include botanical insecticides (made from plants themselves), insecticidal soaps, and certain natural bacteria that are harmful only to the larvae of certain bugs,

Engage in chemical warfare. If none of the previous methods work, your last line of defense is synthetic or chemical controls in the form of insecticides and fungicides. These poisons kill fastest and have the most impact on your garden's ecological balance. In all likelihood, you wont even need them. But if you do, follow the advice of a professional nursery staff person or agricultural extension agent to help you identify the problem and select the treatment. Follow instructions and safety precautions on product labels *exactly.* Safety is a priority, and maintaining ecological balance is a worthy goal, so pest prevention and nontoxic controls are always your best bet Use harsh chemical methods only as a last resort — sparingly, prudently, and. carefully.

Sending Pests Packing
Irritating Insects - Here are some insects that may do their dirty work on bulbs:

Aphids: They're fond of many bulbs, including crocuses, dahlias, tulips, daffodils, and gladiolas

Beetles: Astilbe, begonia, cannas, cyclamen, and dahlias are susceptible, especially when grown in containers,
Mites: They like crocus, cyclamen, begonia, hyacinth, lily, and freesia, among other bulbs.

Narcissus fly larvae or bulb maggots: They bore in and eat bulb centers producing soft, mushy bulbs that don't grow well, if at all. They go for daffodils, amaryllis, rain lily, and others.

Snails and slugs: Prime feeding targets are tulips, dahlias, and lilies.

Thrips: They may hit daffodils, lilies, irises, gladiolas and others.

Annoying Animals

Tasty treats that they are your favorite bulbs may turn otherwise law-abiding animals into serious criminals. Beware the mice, rabbits, voles, woodchucks, and deer that unearth and munch bulbs or crunch foliage and flowers. The following are a few tactics to try:

Plant poisonous bulbs: Daffodils, fritillarias, snowflakes, snowdrops, or colchicums. Not only will animals leave the bulbs alone, but these bulbs may also protect neighboring bulbs.

Use repellents or scare tactics: To stop deer from eating bulbs, some people place bars of deodorant soap (but not cocoa-based soap) around the garden, or sprinkle baby powder. Commercial deer repellent sprays are available. Dogs, if contained, can bark deer away, although neighbors may not appreciate the noise. Vigilant dogs (smaller breeds are easier on beds and borders) and cats can thwart rodents, including rats, mice, gophers, and voles.

Fence bulbs in and deer and rodents out: You can stop these irritating and often hungry creatures; by planting your bulbs in a wire mesh cage. Line the planting hole for a group of bulbs with chicken wire. To hinder mice, use hardware cloth over the bed and remove it when shoots poke out of the ground. Remember that deer don't seem to go in for calla lilies, daffodils, and irises.

Set traps. Some people go for traps, baits, or electronic controls to foil rodents, but you have to consider how much the method will cost (in dollars, trouble, and toxins) to win the war.

Catching a Bug in your Vegetable Garden

Considering how tasty home, grown vegetables are, you shouldn't be too surprised lo find that other creatures want to share in your harvest. The following sections help you identify insects, animals (sorry, we cant do much about your neighbors) and diseases to which your vegetable garden is particularly vulnerable.

In order to fight properly, you need to know your enemy, and insect pests command the largest army of invaders. The following list includes the most common insect pests that are likely to infest your vegetables:

Aphids: Tiny, pear-shaped pests infest many vegetables, including cabbage, cucumbers, and broccoli.

Caterpillars and worms: Moth and butterfly larvae, including tomato hornworms and cabbage loopers are avid eaters and can cause substantial damage to a variety of plants.

Corn ear-worms (or fruit worms): Found throughout the United States, these 1_ -inch long (4-cm) caterpillars attack a variety of plants, including tomatoes, beans, peas, peppers, potatoes, and squash. In spring, night-flying moths lay yellow eggs on the undersides of leaves. The resulting first-generation caterpillars feed on the leaves. You find the eggs of later generations on corn silks; the emerging caterpillars feed on the silks and the kernels at the tips of me corn ears, just inside the husks

Cutworms: Half-inch-long, grayish caterpillars eat the stems of young seedlings, causing them to fall over like small timbers.

Flea beetles: Tiny one-inch beetles that feed on vegetable leaves, riddling them with small shot holes. Various species feed on just about any plant in a garden, including eggplant, tomatoes, broccoli, cabbage, corn, potatoes, spinach, peppers, and sweet potatoes. Adult beetles can spread diseases, wilt sweet corn and their larvae will feed on roots. Adults over winter in the soil and on garden debris, emerging in early spring, and they can destroy young plants quickly.

Japanese beetles: These _ -inch-long beetles will feed on the foliage of many vegetables, including corn, beans, and tomatoes.

Nematodes: These microscopic wormlike pests infect soil, especially in warm climates. They feed on the roots of plants and attack many vegetables, including carrots, tomatoes, and potatoes.

Snails and slugs: These soft-bodied mollusks tend to feed on tender leaves and flowers during the cool of the night or during rainy weather.

Spider mites: Barely visible arachnids often infest tomatoes and beans.

Thrips: These almost-invisible troublemakers commonly feed 011 beans, cabbage, onions, and eggplants, often passing on diseases as they feed.

"Whiteflies: Looking like small white gnats, they congregate on the undersides of leaves, especially on tomatoes and beans.

Not all bugs are bad. Beneficial insects are the police of the garden keeping the bad bugs under control.

If you need to take further action, start with physical barriers that keep the bugs away from your plants. The next step is using pesticides that are effective against a certain pest that are pretty safe to use and that have a mild impact on the rest of your garden's life forms.

The following list identifies methods for keeping common two- and four-footed pests away from your vegetable garden:

Bird tunnels or floating row covers: As you may expect, these keep birds from eating seeds or pulling up newly sprouted plants.

Fences: Fences deter cats, dogs, deer, neighbors, mice, rabbits, raccoons, and woodchucks. Lay chicken wire or hardware cloth over your seedbed until plants sprout to encourage cats to dig elsewhere during the early part of the growing season. Use a slanted fence to keep deer out of your garden. Their instinct is to try to crawl under a fence before jumping it, and they're less likely to jump a wide fence. Keep raccoons out with a fence that's at least 4 feet high, 2 feet for rabbits and 3 feet for woodchucks with another 12 inches underground.

Leave the top 18 inches of the fence unattached to support posts. As the woodchuck or raccoon attempts to climb over the fence, the fence will bead back down under the animal's weight,

Repellents: The most effective way to control moles in your garden is to repel them by spraying a mole repellent that contains castor oil. Pepper spray may deter cats, dogs, and rabbits

Traps: Trapping is the most practical solution to rid your garden of gophers and to control moles.

Allowing your family dog or cat prowl your grounds to ward off wild animals may sound like a good idea, but in reality, keeping your pets indoors or restrained is the best idea especially when large animals are around. Rabies is a problem with many wild animals, such as raccoons and woodchucks, which are ferocious fighters.

The Worst Offenders of the Insect World
—Know your Enemy!

Butterflies and moths don't damage plants as adults and actually help pollinate plants.

The following list includes the worst offenders of the insect world. Many more insects cause damage, of course, and you can get more information about the ones to watch out for in your area from your local nursery.

Aphids: These tiny (up to _-inch) pear-shaped pests come in many colors, including black, green, and red. They pierce holes in plant tissue and suck out the juices, leaving behind sticky sap droppings, called *honeydew,* which attract ants and may turn black if covered with sooty mold. Aphids can proliferate quickly on weakened plants and tend to congregate on the newest leaves and buds.

Bagworm: Adults lay eggs in bags in the fall. After hatching in late spring, bagworm caterpillars feed on the leaves and twigs of many trees and shrubs, especially arborvitae and juniper.

Bean leaf beetles: Adult beetles chew large holes in bean leaves and the larvae attack the roots,

Billbugs: The adult beetles have a long snout and eat turf grass leaves, while the grubs consume the grass roots and lower stems.

Black Turfgrass Ataenius *(Ataenlus spretulus):* These 14-inch-long black beetles lay eggs in turf grass in the spring. The eggs hatch into small white grubs, which feed on grass roots until midsummer.

Borers: Some beetle and moth larvae or grubs tunnel into the wood, canes, and stems of various trees and shrubs. The tunneling weakens the plant, makes it more disease-prone, and can cut off sap circulation, causing wilting and twig or cane death.

Cabbage loopers: The 1-inch-long gray adult moths Jay eggs on cabbages and similar types of crops in late spring to early summer.

Chinch bug: Both the immature nymphs and the black-and-white, one-inch winged adult bugs cause significant damage to lawns and grain crops by sucking the juice from grasses.

Colorado potato beetle: The yellow and black-striped adults emerge and lay orange eggs on the underside of potato-family leaves, such as potato, eggplant, and tomato, The reddish grubs devour the plant leaves, mature, and lay a second generation of eggs later in the summer.

Cucumber beetles: Striped and spotted cucumber beetle species, adult and larvae cause significant damage by chewing large holes in leaves and vegetables and eating their roots. They can also carry viral and bacterial wilt diseases, and spread them throughout your garden.

Cutworms and armyworms: The 1-2-inch long cutworm caterpillars chew through the stems of young plants at night, kill them and then spend the day curled in the soil nearby. Armyworms also feed at night, usually in early summer stripping the leaves from grasses, grains, and vegetable crops.

Flea beetles: These highly mobile, shiny blackish beetles are only Mo-inch long, but they tend to feed in large groups, skeletonizing leaves in a few days time. Adults emerge in spring and do most of their damage by midsummer. Larvae eat plant roots until late summer.

Gypsy moth: The adult moths lay masses of eggs under a fuzzy covering on trees and other surfaces in autumn, producing 2-inch long caterpillars that are gray with brown hairs and distinctive red and blue spots. They emerge in spring to eat the foliage on a number of shade trees. This pest spreads across the country as caterpillars and egg clusters hitchhiking on cars and trucks.

Imported cabbage moth: The white moths have a distinctive black dot on each wing- They lay yellow eggs on the underside of cole crops in spring and early summer. The fuzzy green caterpillars feed on leaves and developing flower buds, leaving piles of green excrement

Japanese beetles: Found mostly east of the Mississippi River, the fat, white, C-shaped1/4-inch-long larvae live in the soil, where they consume grass roots from early spring to early summer. The adults one-inch long, metallic blue-green beetles with coppery backs emerge from the soil in midsummer and attack plants with gusto, stripping leaves, buds, and flowers.

Lace bugs: These insects suck the sap out of the underside of foliage, giving the leaves a whitish or yellow blotchy appearance. Look under the leaves for their brown, sticky droppings.

Leaf miners: The larvae of tiny sawflies, moths, beetles, and flies tunnel through the leaves of trees, shrubs, flowers, and vegetable plants, leaving discolored patches on the foliage.

Leafhoppers: These small, wedge-shaped adults jump from plant to plant, especially when disturbed. The adults and immature nymphs suck plant juices, distorting plant growth and spreading plant diseases,

Nematodes: Plant damaging nematodes are microscopic, worm-like creatures that live in the soil. They usually attack plant roots, but some also attack stems and leaves.

Root maggots: Small flies of several species lay eggs in the soil neat host plants or on the base of the plant. When the maggots hatch, they burrow into the roots killing or stunting the plant.

Scale: Adult-scale insects may have a hard or soft, shell-like exterior that resemble bumps on plant stems and leaves. They suck plant sap and can weaken and even kill plants if present in large numbers. Many species secrete sticky honeydew that encourages fungus to grow.

Snails and slugs; These pests feed on the tender leaves of many ornamental, fruiting, and vegetable plants during the cool of night or in rainy weather. They proliferate in damp areas, hiding and breeding under rocks, mulch, and other garden debris.

Spruce Budworm: These caterpillars cause significant damage to spruce and fir forests throughout North America and can severely disfigure and kill landscape trees as well. In midsummer, moths lay eggs, which hatch into small, orange-yellow to brownish caterpillars. The caterpillars hibernate until the following spring when they emerge to eat the mature and newly developing needles.

Squash bugs: These brown, green, or gray bugs and their nymphs attack the leaves of squash and pumpkins. They become a problem when their population swells in late summer.

Tarnished plant bug; Very destructive plant bugs pierce plant tissues and suck the sap. Their feeding damages the plant, causing swelling, dead spots, bud drop, and distorted growth. The brownish, flattened oval bugs also spread plant diseases.

Thrips: These tiny, slender-bodied flying Insects damage all soft parts of ornamental and vegetable plants, including leaves, flowers, and roots. Infested flowers and young fruits look distorted. Leaves have silvery or white discolored patches on them, sometimes speckled with black.

BOG & POND GARDENING

A bog garden is basically a marshy area with plants that will survive in a year-round moist climate. It is not necessarily a pond. A pond is usually made using a ready-made shell or plastic liner. In a bog it is essential that the soil is kept very moist all through the year. The best are is one that will be low-lying and collect surface drainage. It doesn't take very much water to keep a bog garden moist, and just a trickle will do.

YOU WON'T NEED A HEAVY EQUIPMENT OPERATER

Ideally: to make a bog just dig out about 2 feet of the topsoil. Place this aside and place about 5 inches of smooth rocks on the bottom. Prepare a mixture of half peat and half loam and fill the hole to the top, keeping it level with the surrounding area. Two feet is the maximum depth for a successful bog garden.

OLD POOL LINERS WORK GREAT

Just place the pool liner on the bottom instead of the rocks and puncture it to allow for drainage. This can be used for a bog garden or a pond.

TRICKLE, TRICKLE

If you have a natural flow of water, no problem! If not, you will have to provide a small artificial trickle, which must be just enough to keep the bog garden well saturated.

OPEN THE FLOOD GATES

During the summer, it would be best to allow the bog garden to flood and become heavily saturated for at least

4-6 weeks. This depends on your climate and the rain during that period.

HOW DRY I AM
To allow a bog garden to suffer from drought will probably kill all the plants in a short period of time. Bogs are not recommended for the Southwestern United States.

GETTING THE PICK OF THE LITTER
Most landscape or gardening businesses will have a selection of plants that will do well in a bog garden and provide you with planting and feeding tips for the plants you choose. Color of the plants, planting location and height selection is important. The following are some of the more common plants for a bog garden:
- Lysichitum (yellow skunk cabbage.) 18-36 inches
- Flag iris versicolor 36-48 inches
- Osmunda 24-48 inches
- Hosta 12-36 inches
- Astilbe 18-48 inches
- Primula 6-18 inches

DON'T DROWN THE LITTLE CREATURES
Be sure that your bog garden has a shallow end to allow any small amphibians to enter and leave without drowning and getting trapped.

THE EDIBLE BOG GARDEN
Many plants are edible and have been very successful in bog gardens for centuries. The following are a few of the more common varieties:
- *Watercress* will grow very nicely in areas were the water is about 2 inches deep. The seeds can be

used as a mustard substitute. It should be started by seed or a cutting which roots easily.

- **Brookweed** prefers shallow water and very wet soil. Only the young leaves can be eaten either cooked or raw.
- **Creeping Dogwood** will grow better on the outer edges of the bog, but does not do well if the soil is too chalky. The fruit is edible.
- **Cape Pondweed** grows well in bogs when the water is between 6 inches and 2 feet. Prefers a highly fertilized soil and the tubers are edible as well as the flowering spikes. The tubers are often substituted for spinach.
- **Galingale** likes a marshy soil. The root can be eaten or powdered and used as a spice.
- **Yellow Water Lily** prefers water of 1-2 feet in depth and full sun. The roots and stalks can be eaten either cooked or raw. The flowers can be used to make a tea.
- **White Water Lily** prefers the deepest area of the bog garden and likes the sun and a rich soil diet. The seeds may be roasted and used as you would coffee.
- **Arrow Head** likes water levels of about 1-2 feet in depth. The tuber can be cooked and mashed and is a very popular starch in China.
- **Water Chestnut** likes water 1-2 feet deep. The seeds can be consumed raw, dried or cooked. When dried the seeds can be powdered and used as a flour.
- **Small Cranberry** does best grown in an acidic soil. The fruit is edible and a tea can be prepared from the leaves.

- *Float Grass* is best grown in the shallow areas of the bog garden. The seeds are edible and commonly used in puddings.

HAVE A BUG FOR DINNER
Carnivorous plants do very well in a bog garden especially when planted in sphagnum moss. The ones that do best are:
- *Sundews*
- *Venus Flytrap*
- *Pitcher Plants*

PLANT A PRETTY
Orchids do well in most bog gardens. The most desirable ones are the white or orange fringed, grass pink, rose pogonia and the pink lady slipper. Best to purchase the orchids from a nursery.

STAYING IN CONTROL
Some bog plants tend to do too well and need to be controlled. These include cranberry plants, rosemary, bog laurel, bog bean, horsetails and cotton grass. Be firm with these and don't let them get out of hand.

GETTING POTTED IN A POND
Deep-water aquatic plants can be planted in plastic pots with soil as long as you place small rocks or gravel around the top of the soil. Metal pots may disintegrate and rust. The gravel will stop any fish from bothering the soil. The best soil will be rotted turf. Don't use soil rich in organic matter such as manure.

BULBS

Bulbs are actually storage tanks for nutrients. They are normally planted in the early spring, but certain varieties can be planted at various times of the year depending on when you want the flowers to bloom.

HOPE YOU CAN DIG IT
Many bulbs are very tender and should be removed from the ground before freezing winter temperatures. Bulbs will remain healthier if removed from the ground in almost any climate. If the foliage begins to turn yellow and the plant falls over, it is time to remove it from the ground.

HELP! I'M GETTING WATERLOGGED
The biggest problems that ruin bulbs and bulb plants is over-watering. If the water is left standing around the plant, the bulb will be worthless for the next season.

ROOM TO BREATHE
Planting bulbs in a small pot, then burying the pot is a favorite method of growing flowers from bulbs and makes it easier to remove the bulbs for the next season. When storing the pots be sure that the soil is very dry or the bulbs will rot during the winter storage.

IT'S GETTING DARK DOWN HERE
Be careful not to plant bulbs upside down. The narrow end goes up, which should not have any sign of roots. However sometimes the roots do not show.

FOOD, I NEED FOOD
After you dig a hole to plant the bulbs in, be sure and add a handful of a fertilizer that contains about 9%

phosphorus, 9% nitrogen and about 6% potassium. If the bulbs are not removed just add some fertilizer to the topsoil every year.

I NEED A COMFORTABLE BED
Bulbs should be stored in a brown paper bag that has been filled with peat. This will control the level of moisture during the winter months.

DON'T STORE ME NEAR THE HEATER
Bulbs that are removed from the ground need to be stored in a cool, dry location. Ideally, the temperature should be around 50^0F. When they are removed from the ground cut the tops back and only allow about 2 inches of the stem to remain. Be sure and remove any traces of soil.

I'M NEVER BLUE
Begonias will bloom all summer until the first frost. They can be any color except blue, even two-toned ones. Remember to always stalk begonias. If they get more than 3 hours of morning sun they may burn, so check the area carefully before you plant them.

HEY BUD, I JUST GOT PINCHED
To grow the largest flowers from a begonia plant, just pinch off the smaller buds on either side of the larger one.

HO HUM, TIME TO SLEEP
Begonias will start to go dormant usually in August and should not be fertilized or you will interfere with their dormancy period. They need to have time to store up food for the next season.

I'M REALLY A LATE BLOOMER
Crocuses will usually bloom in the spring but are not as pretty. If you wait until the early fall you will see nicer flowers appearing. Best to plant the bulbs in late summer and allow them to bloom in the early fall initially.

I'M BEST IF YOU CONTAIN ME
Dahlias tend to do better if planted in a container. Add mulch around the bulb to keep the moisture contained, especially if the weather is very hot.

OPEN WIDE
Gladiolas are excellent for flower arrangements. Make sure when they are cut that at least half the flowers have not opened since they will open shortly.

LEAVE MY FOOD ALONE
Daffodils must be left alone and the yellow leaves allowed to remain until they equal about 1/3 of the leaves on the plant. If they are removed too soon you will remove too much of the food supply and the plants will not have stored enough energy.

RING-A-DING DING
Spanish bluebells should always be planted in the shade. They require no special care and will do just fine on their own.

TRYING, BUT STILL CAN'T MAKE BLUE
Tulips can be grown in every color except blue. They like full sun if you live in a northern climate. Late fall or early December is the best time to plant tulips. If the ground warms up before they are ready, they will not do well.

TAKE CARE WHEN POTTING BULBS

Bulbs should never be placed on the bottom of a pot. Always plant them about 2 inches deep for the best results.

COMPOSTING

Composting is layering natural ingredients in a pile is certain mixed proportions. It is also necessary to provide the pile with adequate air and moisture so that bacterial action will decay the material releasing fertilization components for plants. Composting can be done is a specific wooden bin built for that purpose or just placed in an unused location away from your house. **An effective compost pile is usually about 6 feet high about 4 feet wide and about 20 feet long.**

WORD TO THE WISE
Always compost sawdust before you place any in the garden. Sawdust is a low nitrogen and high carbon substance. If placed in the garden without going through composting it may cause a nitrogen deficiency in the soil as it decays. If you do decide to use fresh sawdust, be sure and add some manure to increase the soil nitrogen content.

SOWBUGS AWAY
Sowbugs need to be part of your compost workers. They prefer decaying material to healthy growing plants. Gather up all the sowbugs you can find and make a deep hole in the compost pile and drop them in. The sowbugs will tunnel into the compost and aerate the compost. To increase the number of sowbugs, just place a flat piece of wood on top of the compost so that they will have a place to reproduce on the underneath side.

GREAT MIXTURE
Manure and sawdust: the compost of champion composters. Manure has a high enough nitrogen content

to activate the compost pile and help create the heat needed for the decaying reaction to take place efficiently. If you cover the pile with a plastic sheet it will help to retain the moisture.

THE SECRET COMPONENTS

- Leaves are great since they are high in mineral content, but make sure they are shredded. They can include any plant or lawn clippings.
- Shredded hay: of almost any type.
- Paper: that does not contain printing and cardboard. Both must be shredded for the best effect.
- Grass clippings.
- Any type of plant or garden residue: especially vegetable residues.
- Garbage from the kitchen: especially anything green or vegetable.
- Animal manure is a great addition.
- Miscellaneous residues: such as wood shavings, peanut hulls, sawdust and even coffee grounds.

THE DEVIL MADE ME DO IT

The compost pile should be turned every 2-3 weeks using a pitchfork. The outer material should be placed on the inside of the pile every time you turn it. The inside of the pile will heat up to 140-150^{0}F but after about 3 months it should be finished and the heat level will probably level off to about 130^{0}F.

NATURAL SUBSTITUTE

If you don't have any animal manure, grass clipping will be a good substitute. However, one or the other must be part of the compost pile.

MEASURING YOUR COMPOST

When using compost to fertilize your garden area, be sure to only use about 2 bushels per 100 square feet and only once a year.

EDIBLE PLANTS

YUM, YUM
Flowers can be very pretty, however, there are some that are both pretty and edible. These include carnations, chives, roses, pansies, squash blossoms, sunflowers and day lilies.

FERTILIZERS

ORGANIC FERTILIZERS
There are two schools of thought regarding organic fertilizers versus inorganic fertilizers. Most organic farmers do claim that their produce tastes better, however, most will admit that the produce tends to lose a certain amount of eye appeal. Chemically, plants cannot discern between a nutrient coming from an organic source or a nutrient coming from a chemically prepared concoction. The following is general information regarding organic fertilizers, which do provide well-balanced nutrients needed by the plants.

FEED ME, FEED ME
- *Animal Manure (dried)* – Not the best source of nutrients but does contain a good level of trace minerals. Should be mixed with peat for the best results. The nitrogen, phosphorus and potassium content is about 1% for each.
- *Animal Manure (liquid)* – Most contain the major nutrients but not in high amounts. It is high in trace minerals. The nitrogen, phosphorus and potassium content is about 1% each.
- *Fish Meal* – Normally sold as semi-organic since certain nutrients are usually added. Contains

about 9% nitrogen and 2-3% phosphorus. Best is potash has been added on the label.

- *Bone Meal* – This is one of the more popular fertilizers and has the ability to activate root growth better than most. If you purchase bone meal the label must state that it is "steamed." Raw bone meal may carry anthrax virus, however, it is safe if steamed. Best to wear gloves and a quality mask when using bone meal as an extra precaution. Contains about 3-4& nitrogen and 22% phosphorus.
- *Dried Blood* – One of the fastest acting nitrogen fertilizers, usually used when a farmer feels that the plants need a "nitrogen boost." Best not to use dried blood if you expect frost or are in a rainy period. Tends to wash into the soil too easily. Mid-summer is the latest this fertilizer is usually recommended. The nitrogen content is about 12-14% and the phosphorus content is less than 1%.
- *General All-Purpose* – Should be composed of animal manure, seaweed, minerals and plant residues. This combination supplies the best all around nutrition for your plants. The nitrogen and phosphorus content will vary but should be in very adequate supply.
- *Hoof & Horn* – Very good source of slow-release nitrogen fertilizer. The horns and hoofs are high-heat processed to 140^0F before they are packaged making them safe to use. Needs to be broken down by soil bacteria and should be applied at least 2 weeks before it is needed. Best used in the spring on cruciferous plants. The nitrogen content is about 12-13% and the phosphorus content is about 2%.

- **Potash (rock)** – Excellent source of potassium, which is missing from most fertilizers. Has poor solubility so it will remain on the soil and not be absorbed when it rains that easily. This allows the plants to use the fertilizer as needed.
- **Seaweed (liquid)** – Contains excellent source of nitrogen, phosphorus and potash. High in trace minerals and contains natural growth hormones. Good potassium level of about 3%.
- **Seaweed (meal)** – One of the best substitutes for general all-purpose fertilizer. Tends to be well balanced and has a slower release of nutrients. High in trace minerals and has an excellent combination of nutrients. Higher priced than most general all-purpose fertilizers. Best applied when the soil is warm. Has nitrogen content of 3% and is high in potassium and low in phosphorus.
- **Wood Ash** – Excellent source of potassium and phosphorus when limbs and small trigs are shredded, burned and composted into ash. The level of the minerals depends of the materials burned.

ASHES TO ASHES
Remember to save the old ashes from a fireplace, dry them and use them as a fertilizer in the spring to increase the pH (alkalinity) of the soil.

A GOOD SOIL TO GET POTTED IN
An excellent potting soil is one part of vermiculite, two parts of peat moss and one part of perlite. These are required to give the soil body, aid in water retention and drainage. Perennials need a different type of potting soil

composed of two parts of common topsoil, one part peat moss and one-part sand.

THE EARLY PLANT GETS THE FOOD
Most plants produce their food in the early part of the day. Plants have difficulty producing food as the day gets hotter, especially in the afternoon sun.

DON'T IRRITATE YOUR PLANTS
Watering should never be done at high noon since plants tend to perspire at around this time. The process is called "transpiring." Plants must do this to regulate their temperature from the sun, humidity and wind. If you do water at this time, the majority of the water will be wasted through evaporation.

OUCH! STOP POKING ME
If you poke your index finger into the soil around a plant, the soil should be completely dry before watering. If the soil is the slightest bit moist, the plant does not need water.

PINCH ME, PINCH ME, BUT NOT TOO HARD
Seedlings need to be pinched in their early growth stages to assure that they will have more than one stem. If the seedling is not pinched properly it will not bush out.

IT IS A LITTLE TOO TIGHT IN HERE
If a seedling has yellow leaves at the bottom, it may indicate that the seedling has been in too small a pot for too long a period.

I'M TIED UP IN KNOTS, THIS CAN'T BE HEALTHY
Be sure when purchasing seedlings that the roots are not coming out the pot in all directions. This indicates a root-bound plant and that is not a healthy sign.

HOW BROWN I AM
Seedlings should not show signs of browning or wilting. If browning is evident it has probably been caused by over-watering or a plant disease.

CUT ME, CUT ME, I'LL GROW MORE
There are flowers that when cut regularly they will produce more flowers. These include roses, antirrhinum, cosmos, verbena, viola, nicotiana and heliotrope.

I NEED MY SUNGLASSES
Some plants prefer shade and will grow better if not in direct sunlight. These include begonias, some varieties of viola and coleus.

MULCHING TIME AGAIN
Mulches are the best method of maintaining even soil temperatures in the summer months. They are important, especially in the heat of the day, keeping the soil an even temperature.

VARIETIES OF MULCH
- Buckwheat Hulls – These are lightweight and will not blow away easily. They have the ability to retain moisture very well. Expensive mulch.
- Cocoa Shells – If they become too moist, you may end up with mushrooms. Recommended for flowerbeds. Expensive mulch. Never apply more than one-inch because of its high potash content.

- Leaves – One of the best mulches for adding nutrients and keeping the soil in shape. Keeps the soil moist and cool. Should be shredded for the best results.
- Pine Needles – Do not retain moisture very well.
- Shredded Bark – Comes in different grades. Use the coarser grades for under large shrubs and the finer grades for flowerbeds. Reasonably priced.
- Wood Chips – Only use aged wood chips or shavings since wood chips remove nitrogen from the soil. Aged wood chips are best since they will break down and add organic matter to the soil.

NITROGEN BY ANY OTHER NAME
- Nitrate – This is the form that is available to the plant.
- Ammoniacal – This is available to plants only when it is converted to nitrates by the action of bacteria. The time of conversion depends on the temperature of the soil. Warm soil promotes faster conversion than cold soil.
- Organic – This includes sludge, cottonseed meal, etc. organic matter is slower to breakdown than inorganic matter.
- Urea – Synthetic organic matter that is reduced to inorganic ammonia very rapidly.

STOP! DON'T MOW ME
If the grass is wet or frozen it should not be mowed. A frozen lawn should not even be walked on.

WHEN A LAWN IS NOT A LAWN
Dichondra is not really a grass, but a broad-leafed plant. It is more popular in the warmer southwest climates and

needs a lot of watering. If it gets below 25^{0}F it may die out and need to be re-seeded as soon as the weather warms up. Grows best in light-sandy loam so that water can penetrate easily.

FLOWER ARRANGEMENTS

A LITTLE SEASONING FOR YOUR FLOWERS
A few pinches of table salt should be added to the water in a flower arrangement from a flower shop. The salt will slow down the growth of harmful bacteria.

SWEET & SOUR FOR FRESH-CUT FLOWERS
You can prolong the life of fresh-cut flowers by mixing 2 tablespoons of white vinegar with 2 tablespoons of granulated sugar in 1 quart of water.

A LITTLE DIP WILL DO YA
If you dip freshly-cut flowers into a solution of _ cup of baking soda in 1 quart of water it will extend the life of the flowers.

LAWN CARE

COOL LAWN!
Grass for the most part is a cool weather plant and grows better in cooler climates. If you are going to seed a lawn, remember to seed a lawn in the early spring for the best results. Depending on the area of the country you live in the fall is also a good time.

SPROUTING TIMES FOR LAWN GRASSES	DAYS
Bentgrass	7-12
Chewing's fescue	10-20
Common ryegrass	7-14
Creeping red fescue	10-20
Kentucky bluegrass	20-28
Meadow fescue	7-14
Merion Kentucky bluegrass	20-28
Perennial ryegrass	7-14

HUMIDITY HIGH – DON'T WATER AT NIGHT
If you live in an area of the country that has frequent high humidity, it would be best not to water late at night. Watering just after the sun goes down is ideal in these areas.

THIS WAY AND THAT WAY BUT NEVER THE SAME WAY
It is best to occasionally altering the mowing pattern. Best not to go in the same direction every time you mow. However, altering the direction every time you mow is not the best idea either.

MOWING TIPS TO THE WISE

- Try and mow the grass and keep it at about 3 inches high. High mowing keeps the weeds from getting sunlight.
- Mow as often as the growth requires mowing.
- Never cut more than 1/3 of the length of the grass blade or you will slow down the food production capabilities of the blade.

MIXED GRASSES TO THE RESCUE

To reduce the possibility of diseases attacking your lawn, use a mixture of grasses since diseases attack different varieties. Eventually a turf disease will reach an area of grass that is resistant to the disease and terminates it.

USELESS FACT

In every 100 square feet of lawn you will find about 100,000 turf plants.

SECRETS OF THE PERFECT MOWING

1. Sharp Blades – Dull blades tend to pull and make ragged cuts, which may lead to lawn disease problems.
2. Regular Mowing – At least once a week is recommended during the height of the growing season.
3. Mowing Direction – It is impossible to get a clean cut if you cut your lawn in the same direction every week.
4. Mowing During Drought – Best not to mow your lawn during a drought period because the lawn is in a stress situation.
5. Wet Grass – Mowing wet grass tends to leave wet grass residue, which can damage a healthy lawn.

6. Dry Clippings – Clippings should be raked up within 48 hours of mowing. The lawn disease, thatch is the result of leaving clippings on the lawn for too long a period of time.

TYPES OF GRASSES

GRASSES FOR COOL SEASONS
Bent Grasses
- Astoria - Has fine leaves and is a dull green color, is not very vigorous and tends to get summer diseases easily. It does not like deep shade and prefers full sun.
- Highland - Has upright leaves and is grayish-green in color. Likes full-sun or part-shade.
- Penncross – Has flat, narrow leaves and is bluish-green in color. Prefers sun or part shade. Should be mowed at about _-inch.
- Seaside – Has flat, narrow leaves and bluish-green runners. Very susceptible to summer diseases and should be mowed _-inch.

Fine Fescues
- Creeping Red – A fine-textured, dense turf that mixes well with bluegrass. Works good in shady areas and should be cut 1_ to 2-inches.
- Illahee – Has a very fine texture and is bright green. Very susceptible to summer diseases and tends to grow in clumps. Should be cut 1_ to 2-inches.
- Rainier – This is a very delicate, soft grass with a deep green color. Prefers shady locations.
- Chewing – A delicate grass that is soft and gray-green in color. Does well if moisture and food are in short supply. Tends to yellow in winter.

Coarse Fescus

This is a wide-bladed, clumping grass that is best suited for a football field or areas that receive very rough treatment. Should be seeded at 6-8 pounds per 1,000 square feet. If you sow at heavy rate the texture will be finer.

- Meadow – A very pliant, medium-coarse grass that is dark green. It grows very quickly and is very strong. Should be mowed 1_-inches.
- Alta – A very sturdy grass that is drought-resistant and has a long lifetime. Needs regular mowing and if neglected will get tough. Should be cut _ to 2-inches.

Blue Grass

- Kentucky – A very dense sod with dark green leaves. The best, all-around lawn for the cool-season grass areas. Growth is slow in summer and it tends to grow faster in cool seasons. Does not do well in shade and prefers full sun.
- Merion Kentucky – A denser grass than the traditional Kentucky Bluegrass. Dark blue color and more resistant to drought conditions. Tendency to be susceptible to rust and should be mowed _ to 1-inch.
- Newport – Has the same texture as Merion Kentucky, however, it less susceptible to rust. Should be cut no lower than 1_-inches.
- Delta – Similar to Kentucky Bluegrass and there are no advantages over it. Not quite as dense as Kentucky Bluegrass, but is more erect and stiffer.

- Park – Has very strong seedlings and is similar to Kentucky Blugrass in all other areas.
- Poa Trivialis – This is a very fine-textured grass that is a reddish-green color. One of the best growing grasses in wet, shady areas. May not do well in high summer heat.

Rye Grasses
Does not produce a really tight, knitting grass. Used as a temporary ground cover in the Southwest.

- Perennial – A medium course grass with sparsely set leaves. Does well in most climates and is hard to mow in the summer due to its bunchy growth. Mow at 1_-inches.
- Annual – This is a coarser grass than perennial rye and used mostly as a cover for winter grass over a Bermuda grass lawn. Usually contains some perennial rye and dies out in about 1 year. Should be mowed at 1_ inches.

Redtop
Tends to grow in coarse, weedy clumps in the spring, but will turn into a fine, bent-grass in the late summer. Capable of growing in moist or dry soil conditions and is able to grow well in both shade and full sun. Mow at _ to 1-inch.

Clover
Has the ability to make its own nitrogen, which means that the grass will require fewer feedings. Grows in a dark green color and is very lush.

SUBTROPICAL GRASSES

Zosia Grasses
These are slow-growing grasses that take about 2-3 years to develop a solid turf surface. Work great for shade areas and hold up very well when dormant.

- Z. japonica – A coarse tropical grass that is disease resistant. The grass handles drought conditions well but does require 1-2 years to get a solid covering. The grass grows very well in shade and should be cut to 1_-inches.
- Meyer – The blades are very broad at the base and tend to taper to a point. Looks similar to a high grade of Kentucky Bluegrass when matured. Handles drought conditions well and is very disease resistant. Good grass for high traffic lawns, especially with children. Only grows fair in shade and the winter color is brown. Should be mowed _-inch.
- Z. matrella – This is a medium to fine-textured grass and very easy to maintain. It is resistant to heavy wear and is capable of growing in shady areas. Mow to _ inch.

St. Augustine Grass
A very wide blade grass, rugged, tough grass. Does not need a lot of feeding nor watering to survive. Requires a power mower and turns brown in winter months.

HOW SMOOTH I AM
A lawn bed should be as smooth and flat as possible allowing for a slight pitch to accommodate drainage. A grade that is from 6-10 inches in about 100 feet is not too

much. Once the roots have reached their saturation level the water should run off easily and not be allowed to form standing puddles.

NUTRITION FIRST
Before starting a new lawn it is always recommended to work a phosphate fertilizer into the soil. This is an important nutrient to have in the soil, especially for a new lawn. Phosphates do not move into the soil well after the lawn has been planted.

YOU WON'T FAIL IN THE FALL
The best time to plant a new lawn is in the fall, allowing at least 6 weeks of temperature around $50\text{-}70^0\text{F}$. This is the preferred time and temperature to guarantee success with a newly planted lawn.

DON'T BE A HEEL
When working a newly seeded area, be sure and wear shoes that are flat-soled, tennis sneakers or go barefooted. Never wear shoes with heels since they tend to dig in and leave an indentation that is difficult to remove easily.

SATURATION A MUST
Peat moss is commonly used to cover seeds, however, it does not retain water well. If you do use peat moss, be sure and wet it down and saturate it really well. One successful method is to pre-soak the moss before you apply it to the area. Keep mulch dark with adequate moisture.

DON'T BE A DRAG
One of the more common mistakes people make is to drag a hose across the newly planted area. Make sure that you have a hose that is long enough to do the job.

INDOOR PLANTS

YOU'RE KILLING ME WITH KINDNESS
Over-watering is the cause of most plant failures. Leaves will wilt, turn yellow and drop off. It is easier to revive a plant that has had too little water than to try and save a plant that has been killed from over-watering.

HOW CLEAN I AM
Use an old clean, cotton glove and dip into room temperature water then clean both sides of the leaves.

GETTING POTTED? USE FOAM
Small pieces of foam used in the packaging industry works better than pebbles in the bottom of flowerpots. They don't add excess weight to the pots and tend to retain some of the water more efficiently.

SAVE THE EGGSHELLS
Crushed eggshells should be added to the soil of indoor plants to provide better drainage and some needed trace minerals.

OUTDOOR PLANTS

Many outdoor plants are called "annuals." Annuals are plants that flower, set their seeds and die off. They have a short lifespan and most of their energy goes into producing flowers instead of a hearty root system. They usually grow very quickly and produce a flower the first year they are planted. Biennials are plants that take about 2 years to grow and produce flowers. Many of the annuals and biennials will self sow and keep producing flowers. Perennials are just plants that always continual to self sow and have different lifespans.

Flower carpets that have been impregnated with seeds and nutrients are an excellent method of growing annuals.

NAIL THOSE AFRICAN VIOLETS TO THE GROUND
If you plant a few very rusty nails around your African violets, the blossoms will be larger. The plants like a little iron in their diet.

ISOLATION IS A MUST
When you add a new plant to an existing bed of plants, be sure and place the new plant in isolation for 2-3 weeks before you plant it. Be sure and inspect the plant every 3-4 days to be sure that there are no insects or areas of disease forming before planting it. Even new plants from nurseries can pose a problem.

HELP! MY PLANT IS GOING INTO SHOCK

New plants that have been grown in a greenhouse environment often go into "greenhouse shock." The healthy leaves wilt, there is a tendency to over-water and the plant dies. To avoid greenhouse shock, try placing a plastic bag over the plant for 1-2 weeks and gradually open the bag over the 1-2 week period, just a little each day. The plant will acclimate to the different humidity of its new surroundings.

YUCK! TAP WATER AGAIN

Most of the tap water in the United States contains chlorine. The chlorine is not going to kill the plant but might make it ill. If you allow tap water to remain at room temperature for 24 hours the chlorine will dissipate into the air and the water will be safer for the plants. Cold water also has a tendency to shock plants and room temperature water is best.

I'M THIRSTY, MY POT IS POROUS

If you have plants in clay or ceramic pots, they will need more frequent watering since the pots are porous and causes water to evaporate more quickly. Plastic pots tend to work better if you are using the pot as a hanging pot.

HOE, HOE, BUT NOT TOO DEEP

When you hoe to eliminate perky weeds, be sure and never hoe more than 2 inches deep. Hoeing deep may force weed seeds to germinate, surface hoeing is recommended.

HIGH NOON

The best time to water plants in the summer is high noon since the plants will lose more water during the hot afternoons. In the winter water in the early morning since the plant has all day to lose moisture.

STORING CUTTINGS
If you can't plant cuttings immediately, the best way to store them is to place them into a plastic bag and save them in the vegetable drawer in the refrigerator. Spray a small amount of room temperature water into the bag and seal well. The cuttings should last and still be in good shape for up to 5-7 days.

DON'T SOIL THE SOIL
Never work soil that is too wet or you will damage the soil. When you can squeeze a handful of soil and it crumbles then it is OK to work or till.

OUCH, OUCH, THAT HURTS ME
Never walk back and forth on wet or very damp soil. This will damage the soil by compressing it too much. By compacting the soil you can damage the root system of the plants.

NON-MEDICAL STERILIZER
Potting mixes should be sterilized to kill bacteria and weed seeds. One of the simplest ways to do this is to place the potting mix or compost soil mixture in a clean wheelbarrow. Only place a 2-3 inch layer and cover the layer with plastic bags and leave it in full sunlight for about 8 hours. The mixture should be turned 3 times during this period.

HOLEY, HOLEY
To make it easy to start plants and seeds, just purchase a bag of planting mix or peat and poke holes in the top,

while the bag is lying on its side. Plant small starter plants or seeds in the holes and punch holes in the bottom for drainage. When the seeds or plants are ready to be planted, just plant the entire bag as is.

DON'T TILT YOUR TILLER
There are a number of tips when using and storing your tiller that will increase its effective life.

- Always idle your tiller on a level surface for 1-2 minutes before you shut it down. If the engine cools evenly it will reduce the chance of warping and allow oil to lubricate all parts.
- Change the oil shortly after you use the tiller while the oil is still warm and any dirt or residues are still in suspension. Residues will settle out after the engine cools down.
- When you store the tiller, make sure you close the fuel shutoff valve all the way to stop gas from seeping into the engine or leak on the floor.
- Make sure you always check the tiller for loose nuts and bolts every time you store it.
- Cleaning any residue when putting the tiller away will increase the life of the tiller and reduce the chances of overheating the gear housing and shaft.

PANTYHOSE INSTEAD OF METAL TIES
Old pantyhose can be cut into narrow strips and used to tie up plants. This works better than green metal or plastic ties. The pantyhose expand as the plant grows.

SHAKE 'EM UP

To plant small seeds such as carrot, radish or celery, just use an empty seasoning container with holes that are the right size for the job.

PASS THE POTATOES

Next time you plant rosebush slips, try inserting the slip into the center of a white potato. The rose slips will take root faster.

ROSEBUSH HOLDERS

The old-fashioned clothespins work great to hold onto rosebushes while you are trimming them.

HEAR YE, HEAR YE, FUNGI HATES CINNAMON
Peonies tend to attract fungi, slime mold and mildew. If you sprinkle some cinnamon around the plants fungi will not grow. The active ingredient in cinnamon that stops the fungi growth is called ortho-methoxyannamaldehyde. Research has proven that fungi will not grow on cinnamon.

DON'T BUY FLOWERING ANNUALS
While those flats of annuals in full bloom look great they will not be the best ones to buy. Most of these flats will have yellowing leaves and will not last very long. The best way to buy these flowers is to buy them when the buds are just appearing.

IVY SOUP ANYONE
If you have some small patches of ivy in a location that you don't want to use weed killer on, just pour boiling water on the ivy and that will kill it.

WEED ERRADICATOR
A claw hammer is ideal for removing small tough weeds. Just place the weed in the claw and pull it out.

OUCH, OUCH, YOU'RE KILLING ME
Ground cover should never be planted in an area that has traffic. Almost all ground cover is too delicate to be walked on. Make sure that you make walkways through ground cover area.

MAIL-ORDER BARE ROOT SHRUBS
Be sure and place any mail-order bare root shrubs in a bucket of cool water overnight before you plant them. Be sure and remove any broken or dead branches.

YOUNG ONES ARE BEST
Best to purchase young, small shrubs. They are much easier to grow and will actually grow more rapidly than larger ones, which will be more expensive as well.

WHAT YOU CAN'T SEE
Some plants are pruned before you purchase them to remove dead or diseased branches. If a plant doesn't look right and there is evidence of recent pruning, it would be best not to purchase it.

GET OUT YOUR SPYGLASS
Be sure and check the roots of any plant you are purchasing to be sure that the root system is adequate and not in a stunted condition for that size plant.

COLD CAN BE YOUR FRIEND
Many plants, trees and shrubs have certain chilling requirements. Many trees and plants need a number of hours below 45^0F before their buds may be ready to break dormancy. If the buds do not open in time they will drop off before blossoming. Fruit trees are especially susceptible to this problem in California.

WEEDS

A weed is really just another plant that is unwanted in a specific area. It has similar characteristics as most plants. Some weeds are actually desired in gardens because of their colors. Many people keep certain weeds as part of their gardens.

IT'S A BIRD, IT'S A PLANE, IT'S A WEED CARRIER
Annual weeds can be carried into your yard by birds, animals, wind and even raindrops. They may also exist in the soil and not be activated unless you disturb them by tilling the soil.

BETTER PULL IT OUT BY THE ROOTS
Perennial weeds must be removed by the roots and pulled out completely or they will easily re-root. They normally have underground runners that run horizontally through the soil. The long taproots must be eliminated.

CATCH THAT RUNNER, IF YOU CAN
Weed runners can be as far as 2-3 feet from the plant, It is necessary to dig deep when trying to get rid of some weeds.

KILL THEM WHILE THEY ARE YOUNG
Weeds should be eliminated while they are young. The longer you wait, the harder it will be. Taproots are the weakest when the plant is young and easy to remove. Don't wait too long or they will develop seeds.

THERE GO THE FLOWERS

Herbicides will kill weeds, however, they will also kill all the other plants and flowers if it gets too close to come into contact with them. Herbicides actually cause the plant to die of starvation by interfering with the plant's ability to produce food.

VINEGAR TO THE RESCUE

Before you try and kill weeds with an herbicide, try using white vinegar on them. This method is much easier on the environment.

THE TOP TEN TAP ROOT WEEDS
1. Bindweed
2. Burdock
3. Wild Carrot
4. Chickory
5. Dandelion
6. Dock
7. Horse Nettle
8. Wild Parsnip
9. Pokeberry
10. Swallow-wort

WEEDS THAT WILL RETURN EVERY YEAR
These weeds have seeds that are capable of returning year after year.
1. Beggar's Tick
2. Chickweed
3. Crabgrass
4. Knotweed
5. Lamb's Quarter
6. Pigweed
7. Ragweed
8. Shepard's Purse
9. Wild Mustard
10. Wild Oats

WEEDS THAT WILL GROW WITH RUNNERS
The runners usually run above ground and may root along the way depending on conditions.
1. Creeping Buttercup
2. Devil's Painted Brush
3. Ground Ivy
4. Milkweed
5. Stinging Nettle

6. Plantain
7. Poison Ivy
8. Quack Grass
9. Thistles

PESTICIDES

There are hundreds of pesticides available on the market and most work very well. The following are some of the more common ones. If you have a pest problem in your garden it is always best to bring a sample of the problem to a gardening professional and get their advise as to the specific pesticide and its safe use.

ALCOHOL
Use 70% isopropyl alcohol (rubbing alcohol) to control a number of common pests. Works good on scale infestations, but be sure and test an area before spraying. Best to dilute 1-2 cups of alcohol in 1 quart of water.

ALL-PURPOSE INSECT SPRAY
Grind up 1 whole garlic bulb, 1 small white onion and add 1 teaspoon of cayenne pepper and place the mixture in 1 quart of water. Allow the mixture to stand for 1 hour then strain through a piece of cheesecloth and add 1 tablespoon of liquid dish soap and mix well. Spray on plants and be sure and spray the underneath side of the leaves.

AMMONIA
Mix 1 part ammonia with 7 parts tap water and spray the leaves. Try the mixture on a few leaves to see if any

damage will occur first. This spray works well on aphids, fleas, beetles, scales, thrips and whiteflies.

BAKING SODA
When used in a spray bottle, baking soda has fungicidal properties. It will protect the plants as well as eliminate a number of pesky critters. Dissolve 1 teaspoon of baking soda in 1 quart of warm tap water, then add 1 teaspoon of liquid dish soap. When sprayed on this solution will last a long time and keep its effectiveness.

BLEACH
Bleach is excellent for disinfecting garden tools. Bleach should always be used in its diluted form since it is very toxic. Best to use 9 parts cool tap water to 1 part bleach.

BORIC ACID
One of the best baits to control ants is with boric acid. Works great when combined with grape jelly to attract them.

CAYENNE DUST
This hot pepper herb can be used as a dust to repel onion maggots, ants and aphids. It will also discourage most animals from damaging your plants.

CITRUS OILS
Citrus oils obtained from the peels of citrus fruits have chemical properties that tend to kill or discourage certain insects. The active ingredient "limonene" will be on the label of certain products. Some of the insects that are susceptible to the effects of limonene are the leaf-eating caterpillar, potato beetle, fire ants, aphids, mites, flies

and wasps. One of the best commercial products that contain citrus oil is Aphid-Mite™.

DIATOMACEOUS EARTH (DE)
This abrasive dust has been used for years to kill common pests. It is composed of fossilized silica shells of specific algae. The sharp needle-like projections in DE penetrate the insect outer shell and kill it by dehydrating it. A light dusting of DE is very effective in controlling aphids, caterpillars, leaf-hoppers, snails, slugs and thrips. Best to wear a dust mask when using DE. One of the problems with DE is that it will cause irritation to all animals and will kill the beneficial insects as well.

FUNGICIDE
Two of the most common are copper and sulfur, which are deadly poisons. They will eliminate the growth of fungal spores. Best to follow the directions of a gardening professional before using any products that contain these fungicides.

GARLIC OIL
When sprayed on plants will kill a number of common insect pests, however, it may also kill a number of beneficial insects. If you use it with soap added to the spray it will eliminate more of the beneficial insects. Garlic has also been known to damage certain foliages so you might want to test a small area before general spraying.

LIME
Has been used for hundreds of years to control a number of insects. If you do use lime, you must wear a mask to avoid inhaling the dust. Needs to be re-applied after every rain to be effective.

MINERAL OIL
For the best results using mineral oil it should be added to garlic oil or a soap mixture. The oil actually traps the insects, coats their bodies and suffocates them. Has been used for many years on ears of corn to eliminate the problem of corn earworms. Just apply 1-2 drops of mineral oil to the tip of each ear of corn after the silks have wilted to solve the problem.

NICOTINE
Nicotine is extracted from tobacco and is very poisonous. Depending on the concentration used it can kill most soft-bodied insects. If mixed with soapy water it is even more effective. It is used to kill aphids, mealy bugs, scales, fungus gnats and spider mites. Be sure and wear gloves when handling nicotine since it can enter the body through the skin. It is also very harmful to all animals.

PYRETHRIN
This poison comes in several varieties depending on the insect problem you have in your garden. It is commonly called "Pyrethin" and are used on flowers, vegetables and on greenhouse plants. Label directions for its use must be strictly adhered to.

SALT
One of the best uses for rock salt (NaCl) has been in the growing of asparagus plants. However, table salt, which is iodized is not recommended. Rock salt produced from calcium chloride is not recommended only from NaCl. Rock salt may be sold as pickling salt. If used apply

about 2 pounds of rock salt per 100 square feet of your asparagus bed.

SOAP SPRAYS
This is an oldy but goody. Simmer a pot of water with shavings of Fels Naptha soap. After it has simmered for about 20-30 minutes remove the pot and strain the solution. Allow the mixture to cool before using in a sprayer. Best used on aphids, chiggers, whiteflies, earwigs, mites, scales and flies. Always spray the solution on a few leaves to be sure it is safe for the plants. Doesn't do any good to kill the bugs if you end up killing the plant as well.

STARCH SPRAY
This is another old remedy for a variety of garden pests. A number of starches have been effective over the years such as potato starch dextrin and even all-purpose flour. Just mix 2-3 tablespoons of potato starch or flour in 1 quart of water and to make it more effective add 2-3 drops of liquid dish soap. Mix well and spray covering the leaves on all sides. The all-purpose flour has been used as a dust and gets very sticky when it becomes damp, trapping the insects.

SULFUR
Sulfur is a very effective protective fungicide and is used both on plants and trees. Best to wear protective clothing when applying sulfur. The problem with sulfur is that it may kill the beneficial insects as well as the pests and fungus. Use a sprayer with all plastic parts since sulfur may corrode metal. Instructions for its use can be obtained through your local gardening supply store.

PEST CONTROL

Spraying is one of the best methods of insect and pest control. However, most gardeners do not spray properly. All sides of the foliage must be sprayed, which means the underneath sides of the foliage. Every leaf, every stem, branch of the tree and even the trunk must be covered.

WHICH BUG DOES WHAT AND WHEN

APHIDS & ANTS, BUDDIES FOREVER
Aphids are very small, soft bodied insects that suck the sweet sap from a plant leaf. They can be found in yellow, green, black or even pinkish colors. Some have wings, some don't. They usually live in colonies. Because of the sweet honeydew they produce, they will attract ants and may cause fungus to take hold. In warm weather you need to spray every 2-3 weeks to control them. Ants will carry aphids from plant to plant to allow them to produce honeydew for them.

ROOT WEEVILS ARE EVENING DINERS
The adults feed on leaves and the fruit of the plant. Their larvae feed on the roots and can sever the main roots just below the surface. Strawberries are a favorite of the root weevil as well as conifers, trees and some grasses. The black vine weevils, will munch on yew, shrubs and they love vines. Greenhouses are their favorite hangout. Baits or dust needs to be used in spring when they emerge from their soil home. The dust should be applied around the base of the plant at least 2-3 times.

DIABROTICA PREFERS VEGETARIAN CUISINE
A small beetle with a big appetite. They may be called the cucumber beetle and are capable of doing a lot of serious damage if not controlled. It prefers vegetables but if they are not around they will eat shrubs and flowering plants. They are capable of completely defoliating a plant. Their larvae eats the roots as well. In the winter they hibernate and lay their eggs in garden debris (another reason to clean up well). Check with your gardening supply house for the proper spray.

EARWIGS ARE NOT FUSSY EATERS
Earwigs tend to hide during the day under rocks, boards and trash and feast at night. They leave holes in leaves when they eat, they breed in summer and are more active during April-July. Since they will eat almost anything including cloth and even paper, they are difficult to control. They are best controlled in the spring with a good dusting or can be trapped by placing a piece of paper near the problem area, then remove it after they move in during the day and dispose of them.

FULLER'S ROSE WEEVIL IS MESSY
A long beetle with a snout, that loves to eat the edges of the leaves and leave a trail of black excrement behind. Only works the very late shift in the garden and can do a lot of damage. The larvae munches on the roots causing the foliage to turn yellowish. Prefers citrus and gardenias but when these are not available go to roses. Place the beetles in a jar and poison them. If you are squeamish get a kid to do it for you.

LAWN MOTH IS A FUSSY EATER
The larvae of the lawn moth loves to munch on new lawn blades and will leave brown spots and cause the blades to be stunted. The moths can be spotted in the spring and summer hovering over the lawn at around dusk dropping their eggs. Best to see your gardener for control methods.

LEAFHOPPERS SHOULD BE IN THE OLYMPICS
These hopping insects are green and usually feed on grape, ivy, plum or shrub leaves. They leave whitish stipling after they eat but can transmit serious plant

viruses to a variety of vegetables. They can also carry petunia blight and eradicate all your petunias in short order. They prefer the underneath sides of the leaves.

MEALYBUG ARE COLONISTS
Tend to colonize around the stem or on leaf joints. They are sucking insects that will lay their eggs in a colony. Active breeding takes place in the summer and fall and they excrete large amounts of honeydew, which then attracts ants. Hosing off leaves tends to keep them in check, but spraying a pesticide is the answer or using a soil insecticide from the gardening supply house.

SCALES TEND TO STAY PUT
These are very tiny insects that have a protective shell. They attach to the stem or underneath side of a leaf and will suck out the plant juices. The adults are stationary, but the young tend to move about. They will attract ant since they produce honeydew and can cause fungus to get a foothold. Infested areas need to be pruned and the young crawlers need to be killed with an oil spray or insecticide. Some of the adults will remain in the winter and you will need to spray during this period.

WHITEFLIES CAN FLY AWAY
These are very tiny sucking bugs that reside on the underneath side of healthy leaves. If you bother them, they will fly off. They lay their eggs on the underneath side of the leaf and grow fast in warm months. Leaves will turn yellow and fall off if the infestation is severe. Since they produce honeydew, they attract ants and can cause fungus to grow. To get rid of them you need to use a contact insecticide but begin spraying early in the spring.

SLUGS & SNAILS, THE SLIMY INVASION

They can be tracked down by their trails so you need to hunt and destroy them. They can be found under rocks and foliage and in trash areas during the day. They will hide in almost anything that sits on the ground. They eat at night and you need to hunt them with a flashlight and infrared scope, it is a search and destroy mission that should produce results. Check with your gardening supply house for special poisons, but watch out for your pets. Best to use beer and get them drunk.

GRASSHOPPERS ARE BARK STRIPPERS

Voracious feeds on bark and foliage in the late summer, especially if fields near garden become dry. Prefer warm interior valleys and will lay their eggs in the soil waiting for the next spring to hatch. Spray or use an insecticide or spread bait in the early morning hours for the best results.

ROOT-KNOT NEMATODES ARE ALL TIED UP

These are microscopic worms that are found throughout the western states and attack the roots of plants producing root knots called "galls." In hot weather the infected plants quickly die from dehydration since their root systems cannot supply enough water. They are more active in sandy soil and are inactive in cold weather. Fungicides may work, but little else does.

CORN EARWORM LOVE SILKY AREAS

These little worms like the corn that is near the silk. They lay their eggs on the silk at night. It prefers corn but if there is no corn available there are about 30 other varieties of vegetables they can munch on. Best to apply insecticide in an oil base on the silk. An eye dropper works well and never apply the oil to wilted silk. Remember don't feed any treated husks to your livestock or they will get very ill.

TENT CATERPILLARS HAVE THEIR OWN HOME
These caterpillars make a tent around the bottoms of tree branches. They prefer trees but will attack shrubs and possibly vines if they are sturdy. Their eggs are deposited in the smaller branches of the host plant. The cocoon will not hatch until the spring and should be located and eliminated before then. Best to remove the whole limb before spring. If you wait until summer and they get a foothold, you will have to spray or dust with insecticide to get rid of them.

BORERS LOVE TO BURROW
Borers can be the larvae of moths, beetles, sawflies or wasps. These larvae burrow into the stems of trunk of fruit trees, vines and rose bushes. They especially like almond, cherry, apricot, peach and plum trees. Spraying is the best method control, however, once they appear under the bark it is best to remove the complete infested area as soon as possible.

SPITTLE BUGS GET FROTHY
These bugs tend to surround themselves with a frothy protective coating and are very easy to recognize. Usually attaches itself to the stem of the plant and sucks the juices out. Found on berries, especially strawberries and gooseberries. Spraying with a hard water spray usually removes the pest. However, if you have a large infestation it would be best to dust the areas.

SOWBUGS CAN BE REAL PILLS

These bugs are really not bad and tend to feast on decayed organic matter more than your plants. They will leave the roots of plants alone if there is enough decayed matter for them to feast on. They are more active if the ground is wet or moist. This is a gill-breathing insect. Pillbugs tend to roll into a ball for protection when disturbed and a sowbug does not, which makes them easy to distinguish between.

WIREWORMS ARE CLICK BEETLES

These are waxy, yellowish worms that have a tendency to live in light soils. They will bore into tubers, cut off roots and kill germinating plants. Their larvae can remain in the soil for 2-3 years before they develop into a click beetle. Best to add insecticidal dust into the soil.

CATERPILLARS WILL FLY AWAY

These will eat irregular holes in plant and vegetable leaves. These are very destructive pests that do considerable damage. Best to dust vegetables or just hand pick them off and kill them.

BIRDS LOVE BLUEBERRIES

The most effective method stopping birds from eating your blueberries is to build a frame six inches over the berries and use bird-proof netting. Draping the plants does not work well.

THE DREADED OWL
Fake owls can be purchased in most garden shops and are one of the best ways to keep birds away from your garden. Purchase one with a movable head and you will be surprised how well it will work.

USE YOUR CAN TO PROTECT CORN
Old aluminum cans work great, just make small holes in the cans, cut off one end and place them over the ear of corn.

COMBAT SQUIRRELS WITH PANTYHOSE
Cover corn with pantyhose or old sock after they have pollinated and just before they get ripe.

INNER-TUBES TO THE RESCUE
Old bicycle inner-tubes placed in a cornfield will keep crows and other birds out since they think it is a snake. One tube should protect about 14 square feet.

UNDERGROUND INVASION
If gophers and moles invade your property, just place some oil of peppermint on a cotton ball and drop it down the hole.

HAIR, HAIR LITTLE DEER
To keep deer away from your trees and shrubs, just place some human hair around the area or grate a bar of soap you have been using and sprinkle that around.

CASPER TO THE RESCUE
If you make a ghost with a white sheet and place it on a 5-foot pole with a cross bar, the sheet will flap in the breeze and scare the deer away.

FRUIT TREE PROTECTION

If you hang gallon plastic milk bottles from a limb filled partially (about _ cup) with ammonia the fumes that rise will keep unwanted insects from damaging your trees. Do not use this method after the blossoms show up or you will scare aay the beneficial bees. Replace the ammonia after a rainfall.

DEODORANT FOR DEER????????

If you hang bars of green Irish Spring™ deodorant soap in the trees it will keep the deer away since they don't like the smell. Human hair works great as well.

SLUGGING IT OUT WITH SNAILS

One of the best methods of getting rid of slugs and snails is to use diatomaceous earth (DE). Just sprinkle some around the garden or vegetable bed and they will stay away. It has the ability to dehydrate the slugs and snails and kill them.

HARD WORKING BUGS

Be nice to the hard working bugs that are keeping the unwanted insects at bay. These include the praying mantis, ladybugs and fireflies.

IDENTIFYING INSECT DAMAGE

- If your seedlings are cut off at ground level it is probably the work of a cutworm.
- If you find white pathways on a leaf you have been invaded by leaf miners.
- If you find sticky sap on stems and branches of trees, you have probably been invaded by borers. When they bore into the tree they leave a trail of oozing sap.

- Aphids tend to leave a trail of yellow, spotted or curled leaves. Mealy bugs and white flies tend to leave the same trail.
- If you find a sticky, shiny substance on a leaf it may be caused by scales or aphids.

GET HELP FROM A BUG DETECTIVE
Best to collect samples of damaged area and take the item to your local gardening supply store for identification.

SOLVING THE BUG PROBLEM
- Ants – To get rid of fire ants, just prepare a solution of wet cat food, grape jelly and boric acid. Make a small ball and place it where the problem area is. The worker ants will bring this treat back the queen and it will kill her.
- Aphids – Remove any leaves that have been infected. Ladybugs are your best defense.
- Chinch Bugs – Spray the bugs with a dishwasher soap solution or a spray that contains cayenne pepper.
- Japanese Beetles – They start out as white grubs, which is the stage to catch them in. Check with your gardening supply house for milky spore disease and how to apply it for the best results.
- Leafminers – Spraying cayenne pepper and water should do the trick. Ladybugs may need to be purchased and added to your garden for a permanent cure.
- Mealy bugs – If you spray the area plants with a solution of soap and water in early spring, this should stop the problem.

- Scale – Scale can be gently scrapped off the plant leaves, then gently touch the areas with alcohol. Ladybugs are the best answer here too.
- Spider Mites – Spray the plants with a lime spray or get some ladybugs.
- Thrips – If you spray an insecticidal soap on the plants during the early morning hours; that should work.

IT'S DUSTING TIME
The best time to dust your plants is in the spring and summer. Dusting should be done in the early morning hours to take advantage of the dew on the plants, which help to spread the dust. Sulfur works best when the temperature is high. However, it should not be applied in very hot weather or it will burn the foliage.

SQUIRT BEFORE YOU SPRAY
If you use a water hose and squirt a tree or shrub before you use a pesticide spray, the spray has a better chance of being more effective. If a tree is heavily infested with aphids, the spray will not be as effective unless you rinse the pests off first. Water spraying has always increased effectiveness especially on roses. In fact, dust-covered leaves are more susceptible to red spiders that clean leaves.

POLICING UP THE AREA
Keeping the ground around your plants clean reduces the locations for the insects and pests to live.

PEEK-A-BOO

Earwigs like to hide under boards. If you have this problem just place a board in the problem area and wait a day or two, then lift the board and kill the little critters.

QUICK ERADICATION

- Borers – Infested canes or branches should be burned.
- Earwigs – Catch and then burn in a rolled up newspaper.
- Leaf miner – Discard infested leaves, which may contain larvae.
- Scale – Scrub them off with a toothbrush dipped in summer oil.
- Spittle bug – Hose off the froth and also the nymph inside will be killed by sunlight.
- Tent caterpillar – The silk tents must be burned since they hold the new larvae.

SEASONING FOR LITTLE CRITTERS

To keep small animals away from plants and vegetable garden, try sprinkling some cayenne pepper around. This will also keep cats from using your area for their personal toilet.

PANTYHOSE FOR CABBAGE????

If you place the legs of old pantyhose over a head of cabbage it will keep the cabbageworm moths from damaging the cabbage. The pantyhose will allow light to enter and will stretch as the cabbage grows.

CATERPILLARS DON'T LIKE CITRUS
A substance in citrus fruit called "limonoid" tends to chase caterpillars away. This bitter chemical can be extracted by zesting citrus fruit, then soaking the peelings as well as the ground up seeds in water for about 12-16 hours. Then strain the liquid off and spray areas were you are having a problem.

A HONEY OF AN APHID
To get rid of an aphid problem, just place some yellow plastic lids that have been spread with a light coating of honey. The aphids like honey and become stuck in the honey and die.

GARLIC, NOT JUST FOR VAMPIRES
To keep aphids off your fuchsia plants, just place a few garlic cloves about 6 inches apart around the plants.

GO AWAY YOU MAGGOT
If you are having a problem with apple maggot flies you will need to purchase some styrafoam balls (about the same size as the apples) and paint the red. Then coat the balls with Tack Trap or Tanglefoot. Re-coat the balls as needed.

BASIL, GRASSHOPPERS FAVORITE FOOD
If you have a grasshopper problem, just sprinkle basil around and the grasshoppers will leave all your other plants alone. Basil is their preferred food and they will eat that before your plants.

SLUGGING IT OUT WITH THE SLUGS
The secret to getting rid of slugs is moth crystals. Just sprinkle a light coating around the areas where you are

having a problem. This is a poison so keep the kids away. Another way to eliminate slugs is with white vinegar. Just mix up a half and half solution with the vinegar and water and spray the slugs. Spraying around the plants will also end their little lives.

CHERRY TOMATOES TO THE RESCUE
Cherry tomatoes have a thick skin and a higher alkaloid content. If you alternate your tomato crop and plant cherry tomatoes every other year it will interrupt the cycle of tomato fruitworms. The cherry tomatoes also have the ability to repel the sugarbeet army worm.

WEEDS CAN BE YOUR FRIENDS
It would be wise to leave a patch or two of mixed weeds near your garden or flowers bed. Weed patches are the preferred food and home for many pest insects and even the beneficial insects.

MAY STOP THE GARBAGE MEN TOO
Dogs do not like the smell of ammonia. To keep them from opening up trash bags, just pour a small amount of ammonia on them.

WORKS AS LONG AS YOU DON'T HAVE PETS
Prepare a solution of cayenne pepper and water and place it into a spray bottle and spray along the borders of your yard or areas that you want to keep pesky critters out of.

THE NEW TV WEATHERMAN IS A CRICKET
The approximate outdoor temperature can be determined using cricket noises. Count the number of chirps in 14

seconds, then add 40 and you will arrive at the approximate Fahrenheit temperature.

KEEP FLIES AND MOSQUITOES AT BAY
Basil plants will repel flies and mosquitoes. Plant a few around the garden or place some fresh basil in a muslin bag and hang it around the patio and in the house.

CAST YOUR WORMS UPON THE GARDEN
Worms are hard workers keeping the soil aerated and leaving their castings, which is a valuable fertilizer.

A FEW FRIENDLIES
Toads and frogs, ladybugs, syrphid fly larvae, honeybee, carabid beetle (kill slugs and snails), lacewing flies, wasps (kill caterpillars).

PLANTING

TURN ME OVER AND OVER
The day before you plan on planting any plants, be sure and turn the soil over well. Be sure to also water the soil to allow it to settle.

UNDER A SHADE TREE
Plants in containers should be stored out of the sunlight and in the shade. Make sure they have received adequate water.

THE IDEAL DAY
Planting should be done on a cool, cloudy day if possible. Wind is a problem as well and should be avoided. The best times to plant are before 11AM or after 3PM.

I'M GETTING DIZZY
Staging your new plants is important. They should be placed in the proper location and turned in the proper direction. This is even more important for shrubs since they cannot be moved once they take hold.

GETTING RID OF THE LITTLE GUYS
Make sure that you consider thinning out seedlings to allow more room and the growth of healthier plants.

A SLIPPERY SOLUTION
When planting roses, be sure and add some chopped banana skins to the hole. Banana skins will improve the texture of the soil as well as help the soil to retain moisture.

WHAT A TANGLED WEB WE WEAVE
Before planting roses, be sure and place them into a bucket of water for 1 hour or more so that you will be able to untangle the root ball before planting.

HECK OF A HOLE
The hole that you prepare for the root ball should be about twice the size of the root ball for the best results.

MAN THE LIFEBOATS
If you are going to plant roses in a heavy soil, make sure that you do not add any type of organic matter that tends to retain water. Organic matter tends to draw water out of the moist soil and create a very wet area around the roots. This may cause damage to the root system

FIT FOR A KING

Next time you choose a perennial, check the crown (at the base of the plant) for new growth. Be sure that the crown is in good shape and is not damaged as well.

WELL I'LL BE WILTED

Perennials should be checked well for any wilting condition, which is usually caused by poor watering or drying out too often. These plants will never do well.

GETTING POTTED FOR TOO LONG A PERIOD

If a plant ahs been in its pot for too long a period it may develop algae, moss, a variety of weeds or liverwort. Don't purchase plants before a thorough inspection.

NOT ALL ITS CRACKED UP TO BE

Be sure when purchasing plants that the container or pot is not damaged and cracked. If this has occurred, the roots may have sustained damage.

SEEDS & SEEDLINGS

TIME FOR A DIP

Before you plant seeds, soak them in warm tap water for about 30 hours to soften the seed coat. This will cause the seed to sprout faster. The preferred method is to place the seeds into an insulated bottle, such as a thermos to keep the water warm for a prolonged period of time.

NOT TOO WARM, NOT TOO COLD, JUST RIGHT

If you are starting seedlings indoors, make sure that the water you give them is at room temperature. Cold tap water may slow the growth of seedlings since it tends to chill the roots.

IT'S TEATIME FOR SEEDS
Very hard seeds may need to be soaked in a container of strong tea for about 8-10 hours before planting. The tannic acid in the tea will soften the seed covering allowing for faster sprouting.

LIGHT-UP YOUR BEANS
Bean will sprouts faster if you warm them by placing them near a 75 watt bulb, which will provide just enough heat to help them sprout. Place the beans in a large jar and wrap the jar in a towel allowing one end to remain open for ventilation.

USE A ROLLING PIN, BUT BE GENTLE
Beet seeds will be easier to germinate if you spread the seeds on a piece of wax paper and roll them lightly with a rolling pin. By slightly crushing the outer husk it allows the seeds to germinate faster.

AVOID PASTEURIZATION FUSS
It is recommended that when you start seeds it is done in a sterilized soil mixture, however, you can use a mixture of sphagnum moss, perlite and vermiculite. The seedling should be transplanted as soon as the first leaves appear since there are no nutrients in the mixture.

GENTLY DOES IT, WHEN PLANTING SEEDS
A mistake many people make when planting seeds is planting the seeds too deep with a heavy layer of soil. Most people use a trowel or their hands to cover the seeds resulting in too heavy a layer. Try using a soft bristle paintbrush to brush the soil over the seeds and they will germinate faster.

SAVE THE OLD GRAPEFRUIT HALVES
One of the best seeds holders is half an orange or grapefruit that has been eaten. These make excellent containers to start seeds. Just fill them with soil and plant the seed, then place the holder in the ground when the seeds germinate. The holder will rot away leaving nutrients in the ground around the seed.

JUST ENOUGH HEAT
For fast germination, try placing your seed trays on top of your water heater. There will be just enough heat to speed up germination without harming the seeds.

FORGET THE GROW LIGHTS
The new fluorescent light bulbs that have become popular in the last 2-3 years will work just as well. They are less expensive to operate and will last about 10,000 hours. These new lights provide the blue end of the light spectrum, which is what the plants desire.

PREVENTING DRIED OUT SEEDS
Seeds in flats tend to dry out very quickly. To avoid the problem, just place the seed flat into a plastic bag and check it at regular intervals to be sure that there is not too much moisture in the bag, which may cause mold or disease.

PLANT THEM OR SEAL THEM UP
Most vegetable seeds will last for 3-5 years if stored properly. Place them into well-sealed jar with _ cup of flour or non-fat dry milk to absorb any excess moisture that might still creep in. Pre-packaged silica works well in the jars.

EASY DOES IT WHEN WATERING

When watering newly planted seeds and seedlings, be sure and water gently so that you will not damage or uproot them.

MINI-SEEDS

If you are planting seeds that are as fine as dust, just broadcast them over a smooth-surfaced bed and then press them gently into the soil with a float. They should not be covered with mulch.

SEEDLINGS NEED TO BE PRICKED-OUT

Transplanting seedlings from a seed flat to a larger flat is called "pricking out." This step is very important in assisting the small seedling to better develop their root and leaf system before being plants in the garden. As soon as the seedling has two sets of leaves they should be pricked out. Make sure when you remove the seedling you do not injure the delicate roots.

WAIT FOR THE CLOUDS

If you're going to set out newly transplanted seedlings, the best weather would be cloudy or overcast days. If that's not possible then the late afternoon would suffice. It is best not to place newly transplanted seedlings into the direct sunlight until they have a few hours to recover from the transplanting shock.

WATER IN THE HOLE

When you prepare a hole for a transplanted seedling, be sure and place water in the bottom of the hole, especially if the soil is very dry.

FOLLOW THE INSTRUCTIONS

When planting seeds, it is always best to follow the instructions to the letter. There are many variables when planting seeds and not all seeds should be planted in the same manner.

SOIL PREPARATION

There are only 5 main soil types: these include silt, limestone, clay, sand and peat. They all contain a unique blend of minerals and nutrients. The proportions of these essential elements will vary, however, even in a small area. Managing these various soil types will determine when you cultivate the area as well as the type of plants that will grow there successfully.

SILT

When silt is wet, it tends to pack down turning it into a cold, heavy and badly drained soil, very similar to clay in consistency. Manure tends to help improve the consistency.

SAND

Has the tendency to warm up fast in the spring, which makes it easier to cultivate earlier than most other soils.

CLAY

Very heavy and cold and when compacted it becomes hard. Will not drain easily and is very difficult to work when wet. Usually a very fertile soil that is high in nutrients.

PEAT
Always a dark color and has a high degree of organic matter and nutrients. Must have some type of drainage and usually needs liming.

LIMESTONE
Limestone is a dry soil with a pale color usually with many small stones. Loses nutrients very quickly. Not good for deep-rooted plants.

SALTY SOIL, A REAL PROBLEM
In the west, salty soil can prevent germination or stunt plants that are already growing. This salinity condition; is usually caused by too much salt in the fertilizers used, the water or added chemicals.

FRUIT TREES

THE WINTER SECRET IS MULCH

The colder the winter, the tougher it will be on fruit trees, especially if they are very young. The secret to helping the trees through the winter is to place about 4 inches of mulch around the base of the tree in late fall after you have seen the ground freeze up. The addition of mulch will keep the trees from freezing and re-thawing too many times. The mulch also helps retain the loss of soil moisture.

CALLING TOM SAWYER & HUCKLEBERRY FINN

If the sun becomes strong in early spring the bark of fruit trees do not respond well and bark injury can take place, especially if there is a very cold night after the heat. If you paint the trunk and main limbs with a white exterior latex paint in the fall, the paint will reflect the sunlight and heat just enough to prevent bark damage.

BE KIND TO OLD FRUIT TREES

Fruit trees, especially old apple trees that have had their best days and are in need of extensive pruning to place them back into production can be a problem. If you prune them too heavily it may kill them off. However, if you space the pruning over a 3-year period you will be amazed at the results.

PROTECTION, A MUST

Best to place metal or cement edgings around your trees to protect them from lawnmowers. Best to hand trim around trees. Even lawn edgers with plastic rope will damage the bark of most trees.

MISCELLANEOUS

DON'T USE ANTIFREEZE
Newly planted evergreen trees can be severely damaged by winter temperatures. The best method of protecting them is to staple burlap bags to stakes about 6-inches from each tree. Tie them up well or the weight of snow will break them.

STAKE 'EM IN GOOD
When planting bare-rooted trees, be sure and drive a stake about 18 inches into ground. Be sure that the stake is at least twice as thick as the trees stem it should be about 1/3 of the way up the trees trunk. The stake must be solid in the ground.

MOVING IN THE WIND
Newly planted and staked trees should only be anchored at the base. This allows the tree to move with the wind, which results in a stronger and thicker base and root system. Never use wire or a plastic twine that has the tendency to cut into the tree.

WATERING

When talking to a gardening professional, there is one comment regarding watering that I will always remember. When you water, WATER THOROUGHLY – AND INFREQUENTLY. Over-watering is one of the biggest problems most plants and gardens face.

NOT TOO SHALLOW
If you want a good deep healthy root system, then you need to water deep. Roots will develop deep if there is adequate water, good soil and nutrients to feed on.

A LITTLE WATER DOES NOT GO A LONG WAY
Many people tend to water just enough to cover the ground. Watering needs to be adequate and allowed to percolate deep enough to do some good.

GOING DOWN
Some plants are capable of developing root systems from 2-10 feet, which requires that the water sit on top of the ground and gradually enter the soil. Grapes and tomato plants can have 10-foot deep root systems if watered properly.

WATER, WATER, EVERYWHERE
A 100 square foot garden will require 125 gallons of water to soak down 2 feet. If there is a loam layer then 190 gallons are required and if you have clay soil you will need 330 gallons to water the same area.

HELP! MY WATER IS RUNNING AWAY
Depending on how dry the soil is you are watering, the water runoff may be significant. If you have heavy soil the penetration will be very slow and you can lose 50% of the water. One of the ways to overcome the problem is to aerate the soil by spiking.

GETTING GYPED CAN HELP
Adding gypsum to the soil can help with water penetration. You can add as much as 10 pounds per 100 square feet of garden area.

I'M CHOKING TO DEATH

Over-watering can fill the interspaces around the plant roots and actually cut off the plants oxygen supply. If the respiration of the plant is reduced or cut off it will affect the growth of the plant and can even kill the plant.

I'M BEING ATTACKED

When too much watering is done and the soil becomes low in oxygen, certain bacteria and fungus can become active and damage or kill the plant.

TIMING IS EVERYTHING

The days between watering, is dependent on the depth of the root system. Your gardening shop should have a chart telling you the root depth of your plants. The following is a chart on how many days to allow between waterings:

	Sandy	Loam	Clay
Shallow-rooted	4-6	7-10	10-12
Medium-rooted	7-10	10-12	15-20
Deep-rooted	15-20	20-28	30+

DIGGING A MOAT

The most effective method of watering trees is to dig a small basin around the tree to hold water and allow it to seep into the ground at its own pace. Some plants will also do better using this basin method of water retention. Make sure that you do not scrape away the plants surface soil to make the basin. Basins around full-grown trees should be at least 9-12 inches deep.

SOIL SOAKERS

One of the best methods of slow watering to achieve the best penetration is to use a soil soaking hose. This hose has small holes and only allows a small amount of water to be released.

FURROW WATERING
Scooping out the soil between rows and leaving a furrow for the water is an excellent method of watering. Your furrows should be wide and narrow for the best results. Make the furrows before the plant roots develop or you may damage the plant.

IT'S RAINING, IT'S POURING
One of the best methods of watering is with an overhead sprinkler system. It will spray water evenly over an area. A fine mist spray is recommended, which allows for gradual water penetration. If you use this method, make sure you only water in the morning so that the leaves are dry before nighttime.

SOFT WATER, NOT THE BEST
In some areas of the country, especially the Southwest, the water in soft and contains chemicals that may affect the growth of certain plants. Discuss this problem with your gardening store if you have soft water coming into your sprinkling system.

SECRETS OF FRUITS AND VEGETABLES

GET THE LEAD OUT
If your garden is near a road and you are worried about auto emissions getting on your plants, just spray them with a solution of 2_ teaspoons of white vinegar in 1-gallon of tap water.

BEANS

THE EARLY BIRD GETS THE BEAN

If you want your snap beans to produce over a longer period of time, just pick them when the beans are about pencil width. Make sure that the seeds are just visible. If you wait too long the plant will make the seeds larger instead of the meat of the bean and use up all its energy.

IS IT A BEANSTALK OR A CORNSTALK?

If you plant pole beans next to corn stalks, the beans will use the corn stalk and wind its way up making it easier to grow them without putting up pole for them.

BEETS

IF YOU LIKE THEM YOUNG AND TENDER

Try sowing the beets in a short row about every two weeks and begin four weeks before the last frost during spring.

HOW SWEET IT IS

Beets grown in the spring and fall are usually sweeter than the beets grown in the summer. The cool temperatures tend to cause the beet to store more sugar. If you must grow beets in the summer and would like them sweet, then mulch them to keep the ground as cool as possible.

BERRIES

PLANT THEM OR CHILL THEM
Strawberries need to be planted as soon as possible after being purchased. If you can't plant them, then you need to store them in a refrigerator at 40^0F to keep them dormant. When you remove them, they must be planted immediately or the yield will be reduced.

THE SOUTH WINS THIS ONE
If you plant strawberries on a south-facing slope instead of a north-facing slope, they will bear fruit at least a week earlier.

DON'T WANT THOSE SUNSHADES
If you plant strawberries in narrow rows you will produce more berries. When you plant in wide rows, the plants in the middle of the rows will receive too much shade.

MATURE STRAWBERRIES IN 8 WEEKS??????????
The secret to harvesting mature strawberries in only 8 weeks will depend on the following:
- Plants should be spaced 4 inches apart in rows of 12 inches wide and allow enough room to walk between rows.
- Make sure you mulch the plants and allow them to flower.
- Remove all runners.
- The first year's crop will ripen about 2 months later. The second year's crop will be larger and will come in earlier.
- Forget the old matted row system of planting.

BRRRRRRRRRRRRRRRRRRR

Place about a 2-inch layer of straw over strawberry plants to protect them during the winter. More than 2 inches tends to allow water to percolate through the straw and suffocate the plants. This results in the soil being unable to breathe and allowing carbon dioxide to build up and kill the roots.

DON'T GET BLUE OVER BLUEBERRIES

Blueberries are one of the berry families that do not need a lot of feeding. If you have mature bushes, you should only feed them about 1 pound of a quality cottonseed meal every year to provide you with an excellent yield.

SOME BERRIES DON'T NEED AN OLD CANE

Blackberries, dewberries and most raspberry varieties produce the fruit on "canes" that grew the year before. After harvest pruning is essential in order to grow a good crop the following year. Cut the canes at ground level and do not allow them to remain in the garden. Take care not to damage the new canes that are growing since these will provide you with next years crop.

CARROTS

ARE YOU SUFFERING FROM CRUSTY SOIL?

Crust tends to form on the ground and causes patchy carrot growth. The seedlings are not strong enough to break through in some areas. Never cover carrot seeds with soil, instead use peat, compost or vermiculite.

RADISHES TO THE RESCUE

Radishes have stronger sprouts and can break through the soil easier than carrot sprouts. If you plant radishes with the carrots they will break through the soil crust and allow the carrots to sprout more easily.

CAULIFLOWER

BROWN OUT
It is a common practice to tie the leaves up around a cauliflower plant as it grows to bleach the heads. Instead of the old method, try gathering up the leaves and then place a brown bag over the head. The air will still be able to circulate and will prevent rotting that is common when the leaves are tied.

CHIVES

A WARM CHIVE IS A HEALTHY CHIVE
If you start seeds in the late summer and keep them inside where they can get adequate sun, you will have a nice supply of chives during the winter months.

CORN

DON'T HURT THOSE LITTLE SUCKERS
Corn suckers are the small shoots that grow out from the stalk at ground level. Many people remove them, but the latest research shows that they will not reduce yield and if there is a drought they will send nutrients to the main stalk. If you do remove them and don't remove them properly you may cause diseases to enter the stalk.

FIGS

PUT A PLASTIC BAG ON JACK FROST

Figs do not like frost and the best method to protect them is to cover the branches that will bear fruit with a plastic bag before a frost appears. If you tie small cans filled with a few stones each to the bottom of the bags they cannot blow off.

OKRA

GET OUT THE HAMMER AND CHISEL

Okra seeds have a very hard outer coat, which can hamper germination resulting in an uneven patchy garden. There a number of ways to avoid the potential problem:

- Barely nick the seed coating with a sharp knife.
- Place the seeds on a piece of fine sandpaper and rub them with another sheet.
- The seeds can be soaked in tepid water at room temperature for 24 hours.
- The seeds can be placed in the freezer for about 12 hours, and then soaked in hot tap water for 30 minutes just before planting.

PEPPERS

GIVE THEM SOMETHING TO READ

Next time you plant peppers, try wrapping each plant stem in 6X6-inch square of newspaper. Dip the newspaper in cool tap water before wrapping each pepper plant. When the roots are kept moist it keep away the cutworms.

PUMPKIN

BOARD UP YOUR PUMPKINS
When your pumpkins or squash start to mature, try placing a small board under each fruit. This will protect the fruit from soil-borne bacteria and fungus.

RADISHES

FRIENDS FOREVER
Radish seeds develop strong sprouts that are capable of breaking through the ground. Parsnips do not have very strong sprouts and need the radish sprouts to open up the soil for them.

TOMATOES

TO FLOWER OR NOT TO FLOWER
If you would like early tomatoes, purchase plants with flowers. Don't be upset if the flowers fall off while you are planting them. They are in their reproductive stage and more flowers will appear shortly. If the plants are young and without flowers they will bear fruit later but will give a better harvest.

SPEEDY PLANTING
The easiest method of planting tomatoes plants is to use a bulb planter. It will result in a deep hole and will not take a lot of work.

MOOOOOOO

Dry cow manure is the best fertilizer for tomato plants. It will give you a higher yield. Use about 100 pounds per square feet in plants that are spaced about 3 feet apart.

FIGHTING PLANT DISEASES

HELP! MY BLOSSOMS ARE ROTTING

Blossom-end rotting, is usually caused by too little water or too much water. This problem is common on tomato, peppers and melon plants. If drought is the problem the plants will need at least 1-inch of water per week and keep the plants well mulched. The other cause of blossom-end rot is lack of calcium in the soil. The soil Ph should be about 6-6.5, which can be controlled by using limestone.

MY POTATOES ARE SCABING

To stop potatoes from developing scab, you will need to plant a new breed of potato called the scab-free potato or rotate your crop. If you rotate your crop do not plant them in a field that has been growing turnips, carrots or beets since these vegetables tend to develop scab as well.

FIRE BLIGHT – CALL THE FIRE DEPARTMENT

Blight in an apple orchard is not uncommon. The best method to combat the problem is to spray with a 50:50 solution of apple cider vinegar and water. Make sure you spray after each rainfall, especially if you see burnt leaves.

BLIGHT PREVENTION

Celery is very susceptible to blight and the best method of avoiding the problem is to soak the seeds in very warm

(120^0F) water for about 20-25 minutes before you plant the seeds.

LEAF PROBLEMS

Leaves stippled with yellow
This is usually caused by spider mites who feed on the underneath side of the leaf. When they suck sap, the result is a yellow flecking. Spraying the underneath sides of the leaves 2-3 times a day for 2-3 days usually solves the problem.

Leaves yellowed
Usually caused by whiteflies, which feed on the sap from the leaves. They tend to release a "honeydew" substance, which is sticky and encourages a leaf fungus to grow. This fungus looks black and the best cure is to spray the leaves with insecticidal soap every 3 days for about 2 weeks. Spray the underneath side of the leaves well.

Leaves with large ragged holes
These are usually the result of hungry snails and slugs. Sprinkling diatomaceous earth or cinders around the plants will stop them in their slimy tracks. Shallow dishes of beer will also kill the drunk, little critters.

Leaves with a black coating
A black mold caused by a fungus, which lives on the sticky substance released by aphids and mealy bugs. Best to deal with the pests that produce the sticky, sweet substance that the fungus lives on.

Leaves with powdery white areas
This area is covered with powdery mildew in the form of fungal strands and spores. This is usually an upper leaf problem and causes some yellowing. This problem can spread to other plants if not handled quickly. Thinning out the area and keep the leaves as dry as possible by watering from below.

Leaves that are growing poorly and are greenish-yellow
Leafhoppers carry the disease and spread it through their eating habits. Flowers may be deformed or never bloom. All flowers that do bloom usually turn a yellow-green. Remove any infected plants and see your garden shop for a spray to eradicate them. They tend to flourish in areas that are over-watered.

Leaves spotted and buds turning dark
This problem is caused by plant bugs with red mottling on their wings. They normally prefer the ornamentals and can be controlled by dusting with the chemical, rotenone.

Leaves with spots
Usually caused by fungi or bacteria. There are many varieties that cause leaf spots and if not stopped will eventually spread to the entire leaf. The infected leaves need to be discarded and the area thinned as much as possible.

Leaves rolled over
This problem is caused by the leafroller caterpillar. One of the best method of eliminating the problem is to open the leaf and remove the culprit and then escort them out of the garden.

PLANTING IN POTS

THE RIGHT POT MAKES ALL THE DIFFERENCE
If the pot will remain outside year round the pot should not be made out of terra-cotta or clay if you live an area that freezes.

YOUR POT MAY BE THIRSTY
Many pots are porous and may drink up a lot of the water you are providing for your plants. Be aware that these plants may need more frequent watering. Clay or cement pots are guilty of high water consumption.

GETTING POTTED IN PLASTIC
Plastic pots are inexpensive and very lightweight. They also do not drink water like the clay or cement pots. Fiberglass pots are also becoming very popular.

WOODPECKER CHOW
Wooden planters and boxes are ideal for planters. Be sure, however, that the wood has been pressure treated, if so they will be a better quality and last longer.

GETTING WIRED AND FRAMED
Plant holders made from wire lined with spaghum moss are excellent planters but do require special water methods. Best to spray these and not just pour water in. The moss does not absorb the water very fast. The moss will also take water from the plant and you need to be sure that the moss is good and damp.

DON'T GET SOILED
Be sure and use potting mix instead of regular soil when planting in a plant container. The soil from the garden

does not drain well and if brought indoors, the warmth may cause different diseases to get a start.

THE MAD SCIENTIST
Make your own potting soil for potted plants by using one part perlite, one part peat moss and one part vermiculite. Always add a fertilizer to a potting soil. Sterilized organic compost is ideal as an additive to potting mix.

ROCK'IN THE POT
A layer of small pebbles or rocks should be placed in the bottom of the pot to allow for drainage and to keep the potting mix in the pot. To avoid making a large pot too heavy, try using Styrofoam peanuts in the bottom.

YOUR POT MUST BE HOLY
Never purchase a pot if it doesn't have a drainage hole in the bottom. When you place a plate under the hole, be sure that the plate does not touch the hole and cover it. There should be a small distance between the hole and the plate.

THE DEEPER, THE BETTER
Perennials should be planted in deep pots for the best results. The root systems need all the room they can get. This will also help them make it through the winter months.

IT'S MOVING DAY
If plants in pots are not doing well in the location you chose for them, don't be afraid to move them around and try different sites.

DRIP PANS NEED CARE
Water in a drip pan cannot be left in the pan or it may damage the root system of the plant. One-inch of water, left for a week can permanently damage the roots. Potted plants should be checked at least 3-4 times a week.

IT'S FEEDING TIME AT THE POT
When feeding potted plants, it is always better to underfeed than to overfeed them. Use either a water-soluble fertilizer (one that dissolves in water) or a quality dry fertilizer. Watering washes away the fertilizer so if you can find a time-release fertilizer it would be the best way to go. Wait at least two to three weeks before feeding a newly planted potted plant.

COMING IN FROM THE COLD
Potted plants should be brought in the house in the fall before the first freeze to keep them safe. If possible place them in a warm, sunny location, especially the annuals and herbs.

BIGGGG OUTSIDE POTS
If you have big pots that can't go in the house, you need to remove the plant and soil and clean them out well. The pots should be covered with plastic and boards to keep the snow out.